Career-ology is a great resource for ne\. ....
to launch their careers and young professionals interested in mas-
tering skills for heightened career success. The skills presented in this
book will change the trajectory of your career. Read Career-ology
and take control of your own professional development.

Sarena Diamond Meyer, COO, North America Infrastructure
Services Strategic Consulting, IBM

My experience after college was an unguided tumult of lessons
learned the hard way. Career-ology is the how-to manual that most
of us learn after it's too late, and will set your grad on course with
skills that transcend industries and levels. Reading this book was
like seeing my mental playbook on the page: how to navigate a net-
working event, write an email... even the reference library was filled
with the resources I still use. It took me ten years to figure out what
Chapski lays out for grads before their careers start.

No one prepares you for your first few years after college, and I
had to learn many lessons the hard way. Had I been given Career-
ology upon graduating, my career would have been on much sounder
footing to weather the financial crisis, company closures, and indus-
try transition I went through. Career-ology is the first post-graduate
manual I've read since What Color is Your Parachute *that I think*
earnestly sets you on course in your career. Full of real-world skills and
timely resources, Career-ology should have been tied to my diploma.

Brent Stackhouse, Director of Operations, Administration, and
Special Projects, Mount Sinai Health System, New York

This comprehensive, informative book provides students and recent
grads with a blueprint for landing their first job and being successful
as they start their careers.

Pete Leibman, Author of *I Got My Dream Job and So Can You*

I wish Jeff Chapski had written Career-ology *35 years ago so that I could have read it when I graduated from college. This book is jam-packed with practical, insightful, street-smart advice that simply isn't taught in college, law or business school.* Career-ology *should be mandatory reading for every young lawyer and finance professional. The skills Chapski teaches apply equally to those working in the not-for-profit sector and so this book is also a must-read for young social entrepreneurs.*

Steve Buffone, Partner at Gibson Dunn, Chairman of the Board
of DoSomething.org, Member of the Board of Directors
of Echoing Green and Crisis Text Line

A practical book with very applicable advice and tools. This is a must read for soon to be college graduates or those just a few years out of school. However, it is also a great refresher for those many years into their career, especially the advice on networking. The "hook" is a great concept to prompt follow up questions or comments in response to "What do you do?"

Carol McNerney, SVP, Marketing Strategy,
Insights and Operations, Pitney Bowes

Career-ology *is full of excellent advice and insightful tips for professionals who are starting their careers. In his book, Chapski highlights the skills that are essential for professionals working in all levels of government, politics, and the non-profit sector, among other industries. Developing these skills were a key component of my early career success, and continue to guide my thinking today.*

Steven G. Glickman, Adjunct Assistant Professor,
Georgetown University and Former Director for International
Economic Affairs, National Security Council at The White House

Career-ology *is the secret manual for how to succeed in the workplace. In this digital age, it's too easy to forget that personal skills, communication and the like are the critical difference in getting ahead in the real world. Even peak performers need to understand the "soft skills" that enable rapid advancement and set a person up for the opportunities that their career can provide.*

Jeremy Kagan, founder and CEO of Pricing Engine,
Professor of Digital Marketing at Columbia Business School,
and corporate trainer and consultant

Read this book! Career-ology *provides great practical advice for both the recent college graduate as well as more seasoned professional looking for a refresher. Jeff highlights essential career skills that every professional needs to know. Right from the start the first chapter, Accelerating Your Career Experience, will certainly help job seekers differentiate themselves from the crowd. The skills introduced in the succeeding chapters are the building blocks for a successful career and will serve readers throughout their professional lives.*

Karen Holden, Principal, International Tax Services,
Ernst & Young LLP

Chapski delivers the right stuff for today's career chase!

Roderick von Lipsey, Managing Director of a private
wealth management firm. Retired Lieutenant Colonel
in the United States Marine Corps

To my wife, Jennifer, and my son, Reid.

You make my life better every day.

CAREER -OLOGY

THE ART AND SCIENCE OF A SUCCESSFUL CAREER

JEFF CHAPSKI

LONDON AND WHITE
NEW YORK

Rights and Permissions: jeff@career-ology.com

Designer: Cindy Kiple

Editors: Sallie G. Randolph, Catherine A. Carey, John R. Randolph

ISBN: 978-0-9915213-0-2
LCCN: 2014960324

Publisher's Cataloging-in-Publication Data

Chapski, Jeff.

Career-ology : the art and science of a successful career / Jeff Chapski. -- New York : London and White, 2015.

pages ; cm.

ISBN: 978-0-9915213-0-2
Includes bibliographical references.
Audience: Recent college graduates and new professionals in the first five years of their career.
Summary: This book provides an overview of the key skills that serve as the foundation for professional development, including public speaking and presentation, professional networking, sales and negotiation, navigating the organization, business etiquette, personal branding, and executive presence. For each skill there is a list of specially selected resources for further exploration and study, including other books, blogs, videos, online and offline training. Each chapter includes actionable next steps. --Publisher.

1. Success in business. 2. Career development. 3. Business networks. 4. Social networks. 5. Business writing. 6. Business presentations. 7. Negotiation in business. 8. Sales. I. Title. II. Title: Careerology.

HF5386 .C4944 2015   2014960324

650.1--dc23   1503

London and White
PO Box 2880, Grand Central Station
New York, NY 10163

First Edition

Printed in the United States of America

TABLE OF CONTENTS

PREFACE

The original idea for this book began almost 20 years ago. After graduating from Georgetown University, I began working on Wall Street for J.P. Morgan. I was hired as part of the analyst-training program and spent the first three months of my employment learning about the bank's history, business philosophy, products, lines of business, and senior management. The program also included instruction in business writing, presentation skills, and public speaking, all of which served as a valuable foundation for my career.

After my first year at the bank, I was asked to participate in the on-campus recruiting initiative to interview candidates for the following year's training program. For the next several years, I would return to campus to help with the information sessions and interview college seniors. The students waiting in the lobby of the career center reminded me how nervous I had been when I was interviewing for my first job after college.

During my fifth year of on-campus recruiting, I reflected on how much I had learned since the beginning my career. I was on a flight home after a full day of interviewing when I did a self-inventory of all the professional skills I had acquired through my five years of "on-the-job" training.

I wondered where I would be in my career if I had acquired these professional skills earlier. What if I and other new professionals had these skills at the start of our careers? What if there were a book that highlighted the most important professional skills and concepts needed in the first five years? And the idea for this book was born!

My undergraduate degree in finance from Georgetown University and the analyst-training program at J.P. Morgan certainly provided me a solid foundation. But I was on my own to identify and acquire the professional skills I needed at the start of my career. With some guidance, but mostly on my own, I had to learn how to network with other professionals. I had to learn about international business etiquette, and how to "sell" my ideas to my boss and prospective clients. I wished I had learned these skills sooner. I wished I had understood how important these skills are.

Career-ology focuses on the most important skills and concepts for the first five years of your career. Acquiring and mastering these skills early will change the trajectory of your career. These are not the only skills you need, but they are important for everyone—no matter your field, industry, or profession.

The transition from college to career is one of the biggest transitions you'll ever make. This book will provide you guidance for your own professional development and help you establish a strong foundation of skills for a successful career.

1

THE ART AND SCIENCE OF A SUCCESSFUL CAREER

An Introduction to Career-ology

I'm a great believer in luck and I find the

harder I work, the more of it I have.

THOMAS JEFFERSON

There is not a more appropriate quote to begin this book or a more true statement as it relates to your career—the harder you work, the more luck you will have. While working hard is important, it is not enough. You must also work smart.

This book is about working smart. Working smart means being deliberate about acquiring the skills and knowledge to maximize your chance for a successful career—no matter how you define success. To do your job well, of course, there are important skills and knowledge directly related to your day-to-day work. Most new professionals will focus their time and effort on this. But your success depends on more. You will need to acquire skills beyond those your job requires.

Your professional development is as much an art as it is a science. Some career skills require mastering a set of facts or rules and implementing them. For example, business writing and etiquette are straightforward skills. Other career skills such as understanding the dynamics of your organization and exploring your own emotional quotient are more of an art.

This book is. . . and this book is NOT. . .

The purpose of this book is to provide an overview of the key professional skills and concepts that are important as you begin your career. It is designed to help you focus on the areas of your career development that will serve as a foundation for the rest of your career.

This book is NOT an exhaustive treatment of each skill or concept. There are hundreds (or thousands) of books, blogs, seminars, and online resources dedicated to each. There is no way to go into depth on each skill within the confines of a single chapter. Instead, each chapter will focus on the key points of each skill, highlight the relevance of the skill to your career, and point to additional resources that you may find helpful.

For example, instead of discussing every aspect of public speaking, the *Career-ology* chapter will provide some advice on beginning to acquire this skill, explain why this skill is important for all new professionals, provide a list of the best resources (books, websites, tools, blogs) for further study, and suggest specific steps you can take. Each chapter is organized in the same way. Each is based on my own research and professional experience along with the experience of my colleagues and peers.

This book is meant to be most helpful at the beginning of your professional development. It is meant to serve as a foundation for the skills that will make a difference in your long-term career success.

Success is how you define it

There are many references to "success" or a "successful career" throughout this book. Let's be clear from the start. This book defines success however YOU define success. There are no preconceived notions of what success means. Everyone defines success in his or her own way. ⚒ (This symbol indicates additional information at www.career-ology/link-library).

A larger paycheck may mean success for some. For others it could mean a promotion, a more impressive title, or a move up the corporate ladder. Or it could mean being an entrepreneur, a solo medical practitioner, an artist, a politician, a military officer, a professional musician, or a teacher. Still others may equate success with flexible hours, part-time work, or working remotely. No matter how you define success, the skills and concepts in this book apply to you and to your career.

Why you should read Career-ology

This book is for college students preparing to start their careers and for new professionals who have graduated in the past five years or so. It will provide an overview of the foundational skills and concepts that all professionals need to acquire.

In today's competitive, global economy, managing your own career is not an option—it is a necessity! Many factors and trends outside of your control may impact your career. Here are some:

- Shortened tenure. According the U.S. Bureau of Labor Statistics, the average job tenure for the American worker is 4.6 years. That means that average workers will hold more than ten jobs throughout their careers.

- Flexible work patterns. Many careers will be non-linear. They might shift from full-time employment to consulting work, from large organization to start-up, or from corporate to non-profit, NGO, or government.

- High-impact disruptions. One or more of these disruptions will affect you. Aside from the disruptions inherent in your specific industry or profession, they could include an economic downturn (or upturn), geopolitical upheaval, or advances in technology.

You must focus on your own career and professional development. Acquire and practice skills that you can apply to new roles, industries and opportunities. Build a portfolio of your work and credentials that demonstrate your growing competence and expertise.

If you have any doubts about whether you should read this book, consider these common misunderstandings:

Myth #1: I will get these skills from my employer and as part of my day-to-day job.

You will probably not receive training in all of these skills. Even if you do, how will you continue to hone them once the specific training is complete? If your employer does provide this type of training, your colleagues are also being trained. How will you differentiate yourself?

Myth #2: My job or career is _____ . (Fill in the blank with your position). The skills in this book don't apply in my situation.

The skills and concepts presented in this book apply to all industries, professions, and roles—from entry-level to the C-suite. You may use some skills more frequently than others, but they are all important.

Myth #3: I already know this "stuff."

You may be have been introduced to these skills and concepts. You may even have acquired a working knowledge, but you have not mastered these skills as a new professional. Most successful professionals will say they practice and improve their skills throughout their entire careers. Professionals who believe they are finished learning will not be successful. Those who believe in and practice lifelong learning, however, will always find opportunities and success. Approaching your career with the right mindset could make the difference between simply having a job and having a successful career.

Myth #4: I took a public speaking or a business writing class while in college. I don't need those chapters.

See answer to *Myth #3* above.

Why these skills and concepts?

The skills and concepts in this book are important for professionals in every industry. They will be critical throughout your entire career. The following is a brief overview:

- Professional networking. The secrets of networking can transform it from a chore to an enjoyable experience.

- Business writing. The ability to clearly articulate your ideas in writing (anything from a simple Tweet to a 100-page technical report) is essential.

- Public speaking and presenting. The ability to stand up and present your ideas clearly and concisely is also essential. There is no avoiding it! You will have to be able to communicate ideas to as few as two people or to a room full of 200 or more.

- Sales and negotiating. Everyone is in sales no matter his or her job!

- Organizational awareness. Understanding the people you work with and the unwritten rules they follow will give you a solid career edge.

- Creating your personal brand. Your style and behavior can enhance your personal identity as a professional.

- Developing your executive presence. Projecting a presence of leadership, displaying grace under pressure, and creating the desire in others to get the job done will enhanced your career and your life in many ways.

Building blocks of leadership

The skills and concepts in this book are the foundation of leadership. Think of a great leader and rate his or her abilities on a scale of one to ten against the list of skills above. Chances are the leader you selected rated highly.

You can demonstrate the qualities of a leader without having direct reports. You don't need a title or an organizational chart either. A true leader is a person whom others will follow regardless of the authority of a title or the incentive of a paycheck. It might take a lot more to be an outstanding leader, but these skills and concepts are an excellent place to begin your journey.

People matter most

The people with whom you work—your colleagues, customers, clients, constituents, shareholders, patients, teammates, and partners—are the single most important element of your career. The quality of your relationships with people is directly related to your long-term career success. People are the common thread in all of the skills and concepts presented in this book.

Career-ology will teach you how to communicate with others in writing and spoken form. It will teach you how to persuade and influence people to adopt your viewpoint. It will explain how to continuously develop and cultivate relationships with the people in your company and in your professional networks. It will show you how to understand people and their roles in relation to your own. It will teach you how to begin to manage the perception that others have of you. Finally, it will help you discover your own strengths and weaknesses as you interact with other people at work.

How to use Career-ology

As an overview of the foundational skills and concepts that will increase your chances of a successful career, *Career-ology* is meant to be a reference. Read the chapters in any order that makes sense to you. For example, if your present job involves making sales presentations to clients, you might want to focus on "Public Speaking and Presentation Skills" first. If you are interested in improving the working relationships with your co-workers, you can read Your "Executive Presence".

Even if you use the book as a reference, I hope you will also read each chapter. While some of these skills may be more important to you than others today, all the skills will be important at some time in your career.

Hyperlinks

In the print version of *Career-ology*, the ✘ symbol represents a hyperlink that points to additional supporting material, data, or other related information. There are dozens of hyperlinks indicated throughout the book. Clickable hyperlinks are maintained in an online library at www.career-ology.com/link-library. The idea for these hyperlinks and Link Library is borrowed directly from Guy Kawasaki's book, *APE: How to Publish a Book.* (Thanks, GK. Awesome idea!).

There is a list of Additional Resources at the end of each chapter. I believe these resources are among the best available. These resources will help as you continue to build upon what you learned in the chapter. You may identify other resources that you like as well. Be sure to share what you find with other readers on the Careerology Facebook Page at www.facebook.com/careerologybook.

Last, but definitely not least, this book is action-oriented. The momentum you create by taking even a single action after learning a new concept or idea will help you retain that information. Each chapter includes suggested next steps and will help you put that chapter's advice into practice. Take at least one specific action immediately after reading each chapter. That momentum will make a difference.

Are you ready to get started?

Let's go!

2

ACCELERATE YOUR CAREER EXPERIENCE

Experience is one thing you can't get for nothing.

OSCAR WILDE

In this chapter, you will learn:

- That there is an inherent flaw in the way experience is measured that you can use to your advantage.

- How to use the Career Experience Equation.

- That accelerating your career experience is a simple, yet powerful, way to achieve your career goals in a shorter time.

What is career experience?

The terms "job experience" and "career experience" are ubiquitous and yet there is often a flaw in the way experience is used to measure a person's skills and abilities. A commonly used working definition of the term is "knowledge and skills acquired over time." Experience also describes a person's readiness for a job, a new role, a raise, or a promotion. Experience is most commonly measured in years. "She has ten years of experience in pharmaceutical sales" or "he has two years of experience in website design" are examples.

There is an inherent flaw in the way experience is measured. Keep reading to learn how you can use this flaw to your advantage.

THE DEFINITION OF "EXPERIENCE"

Webster defines experience as "Practical knowledge, skill, or practice derived from direct observation of or participation in events or in a particular activity or the length of such participation." Example: He has ten years experience in the job.

Oxford Dictionaries Online defines experience as "The knowledge or skill acquired over a period of time, especially that gained in a particular profession by someone at work." Example: The company is looking for candidates with the necessary experience.

"Experience" appears in nearly every job posting, an indication of the importance that is attached to this specific word in career-related qualifications. Read the sample job postings below, and note the years of experience that are required in each.

Banking Relationship Manager:

☐ Bachelor's degree in Business Administration or related field required.

☐ Minimum of 3 years sales experience.

☐ Minimum of 3 years managing business banking or commercial relationships preferred.

Senior Marketing Manager:

☐ 5+ years experience in database marketing analysis, including analytics, direct marketing test design, response analysis, ROI analysis, segmentation analysis, customer profiling, etc.

☐ 5+ years experience in email marketing strategy and knowledge of database querying tools and analytical platforms supporting database marketing.

☐ Creative thinking, exceptional analytical skills coupled with solid business foundation, particularly in database and email marketing.

☐ MBA preferred.

The term experience appears in nearly every job post, but what does it really mean? What are employers looking for?

The Career Experience Equation

To reveal the inherent flaw in the way experience is usually measured, let's take a deeper look at the components of career experience. The four components of career experience are tenure, skills, personal brand (PB), and executive presence (EP).

Career Experience = Tenure + Skills + PB + EP

Tenure = the number of years in a specific job, role, or industry.

Skills = the professional skills and concepts you've acquired.

PB = the level of your personal brand.

EP = the level of your executive presence.

Let's examine each of these components.

TENURE

Tenure is as straightforward as it sounds. It is the length of time (generally expressed in the number of years) spent in a specific job, role, or industry. Tenure is the only component of experience that most people consider. For example, a web designer who has been working for three years is generally considered to have three years experience. Likewise, a lawyer who has been practicing criminal defense for five years is said to have five years experience in his or her area of practice.

If experience were measured only by the passing of time, then the examples above would be accurate.

SKILLS

In the Career Experience Equation, skills refer to all of the relevant skills, concepts, and knowledge that you aquire over a given period of time. The key skills and concepts covered in chapters three to nine of *Career-ology* include:

- Networking

- Business writing

- Public speaking and presenting

- Selling

- Negotiating

- Navigating your organization

- Personal branding

- Executive presence

In addition to the skills and concepts in this book, there are other skills and concepts that may be part of your career experience. ✖ The following is a partial list:

- Teamwork

- Team motivation

- Project management

- Time management

- Conflict resolution

- Decision making

- Problem solving

- Task prioritization

- Organization

- Managing up

- Statistical analysis

- Meeting management

- Brainstorming

- Facilitation

- Critical thinking

- Budgeting and forecasting

- Strategic planning

- Change management

- Delegation

Neither list includes the technical or specific skills of every job. Depending on your profession, industry, role, and function, you will use some of these skills more than others.

While you can't increase the rate at which you add to your tenure, you can increase the rate at which you acquire and master new skills, concepts, and knowledge. This is where you can use the common flaw in the way experience is measured to your advantage.

PERSONAL BRAND

Your personal brand (PB) in the workplace is how you define yourself as a professional and how you convey that definition to others. Equally important, your personal brand is how colleagues and clients see you as a professional. There may be a gap between how you define your personal brand and how others perceive it. That's important to keep in mind. Personal brand is not measured in years and therefore you can develop this associated skill at whatever rate you choose. Personal brand is covered in Chapter 9.

EXECUTIVE PRESENCE

Executive presence (EP), the fourth component of the Career Experience Equation, is not a single specific skill. EP is a combination of skills, qualities, and knowledge. An important aspect of executive presence is Emotional Intelligence (EI). Emotional Intelligence (EI) is "the ability to identify, assess and control the emotions of oneself, of others, and of groups" (A Dictionary of Psychology, Coleman). EI explains why people with average intelligence are easily able to outperform those with superior intelligence quotient (IQ) scores. Executive presence is an important part of the Career Experience Equation.

Like skills and personal brand, your executive presence is not measured in years. With deliberate action, you can accelerate the rate of your development in this area. A professional who has been working for five years can demonstrate the same level of executive presence as a person who has been working for ten years. Executive presence is covered in more detail in Chapter 10.

How do you accelerate your career experience?

To accelerate your own career experience, focus on the aspects of the Career Experience Equation that are not specifically linked with time—skills, personal brand, and executive presence. You can proactively acquire and develop these skills in a way that will add to your level of experience when compared with your peers.

The concept of accelerating your career experience is simple, but don't confuse simple with easy. You can apply diligence and discipline to acquire and refine the professional skills that will help you stand out. It is up to you to find the training resources and opportunities to practice these skills.

Consider a sports example: Two tennis players, Jane and Mary, are both new to the sport. Jane and Mary started with the same number of lessons from the same tennis pro. Both have the same level of athletic and physical ability. After completing her lessons, Jane continued to practice three days a week. She worked on specific skills, including her serve and backhand, and worked on her general physical conditioning. Mary's practice consisted of an occasional match with friends. After two years, Jane and Mary each have two years of experience playing tennis. But it's easy to see who is the better player, right?

The analogy extends beyond athletics. A similar scenario is applicable to learning a musical instrument, acting on stage, driving a car, or developing your own career. The concept of practicing and mastering professional skills is lost on many people in the workforce, but it doesn't have to be lost on you. Practice will make the difference.

Why accelerating your career experience is important

In today's competitive workplace, nurturing your key professional skills will give you a decided advantage.

Consider this: You and your co-worker, Bob, are hired at the same time to do the same job in the same business unit of a large multi-national corporation. You and Bob attended the same college, earned the same degree, and achieved the same grade point average. On paper, you are equally matched employees. How will you set yourself apart from Bob? You can stand out from all the other Bobs out there by accelerating your career experience.

You determine that business writing and public speaking are important skills given your current role with this organization. In order to improve your business writing skills, you take an online business writing class. You also attend Toastmasters meetings two times a month to practice your public speaking skills.

In addition, you join a group of alumni who work in the same industry. This group meets periodically to discuss topics relevant to the industry and to network. You also join another professional association within your industry and help organize the annual conference. Your commitment to the professional association gives you direct contact with the director of the association and other industry leaders.

After a couple of years, who has more professional experience, you or Bob?

How to accelerate your career experience

It's worth repeating – accelerating your career experience is a simple idea, but it is not easy to apply. Here are some guidelines to help you accelerate your career experience:

Habit. Make it a habit early in your career to focus on your own professional development. ✻

Practice. Practice the skills that you need for success with the dedication of a professional athlete, Hollywood actor, or a rock star. ✻

Discipline. Schedule a regular time for your professional development and stick to it. Committing to your plan may be the biggest challenge, but if you do, the results will follow. ✻

ACCELERATE YOUR CAREER EXPERIENCE: NEXT STEPS

1. Decide. Decide to focus on acquiring and mastering the career skills that will make you successful. Take responsibility for your own professional development by accelerating your career experience. This is the MOST important Next Step in the entire book!

2. You need thirty to sixty minutes of uninterrupted time for this exercise. Put your phone away and turn off the computer. On a blank sheet of paper, you are going to write two lists. For the first list, write the top ten most important career skills and concepts that would make you more successful in your current role. For the second list, write the ten most important career skills and concepts you need to acquire for the job, role, or position that you want to have in two years. Not sure? Look at your boss's boss, successful colleagues, or ask people in your professional network for their opinions. Rate your current level of proficiency (one to ten, where 10 is outstanding) for each skill you identified.

3. Select one skill or concept that will help in your current role and one skill that will help in your future role and begin applying what you learned in this chapter.

4. Review the Additional Resources for this chapter. The ideas and lessons in these books reinforce the conceptual framework for accelerating your career experience.

5. Take action. This book is designed to prompt you, the reader, to take action—not just read the pages. I guarantee that readers who take action will achieve greater career success than those who don't.

ADDITIONAL RESOURCES ✗

The Power of Habits: Why We Do What We Do In Life and Business
by Charles Duhigg

Why? You will dive deep into the science of habits and learn how to harness the power of habits to accelerate your career experience. Duhigg, an award winning business journalist, also explores institutional habits and the idea of keystone habits that can be used to turn around organizations like Alcoa, the Fortune 500 manufacturing company, or products like P&G's Febreze air freshener.

Practice Perfect: 42 Rules for Getting Better at Getting Better
by Doug Lemov, Erica Woolway, Katie Yezzi

Why? If you question the value of practice in your career, this is a MUST read. Many of the rules will show you how to set up practice routines for skills where the solution is not obvious. Rules most applicable to accelerating your career experience include: #1 Encode Success, #4 Unlock Creativity . . . With Repetition, #7 Differentiate Drill From Scrimmage, #9 Analyze the Game, and #10 Isolate the Skill.

Mastery: The Keys to Success and Long-Term Fulfillment
by George Leonard

Why? This book is a bit esoteric, but I've included it here because "practice" and "mastery" are at the core of accelerating your career experience. I first learned of Leonard's book through my own Aikido practice and really admire his Yoda-like lessons. These lessons transcend career and include all aspects of life.

Eat That Frog
by Brian Tracy

Why? Written by the international best-selling author and leader in professional development, *Eat That Frog* will help you jumpstart your professional development (or any other task in your work) with twenty-one proven methods and techniques. These methods are integral to accelerating your career: #7 Focus on Key Result Areas, #10 Take It One Oil Barrel at a Time, #11 Upgrade Your Skills, #13 Identify Your Key Constraints, #21 Single Hand Every Task.

3

PROFESSIONAL NETWORKING

Dig a well before you are thirsty.

CHINESE PROVERB

In this chapter, you will learn:

- Why networking is important to your success.
- What networking is and what it is not.
- The secret to making networking fun.
- Where to find high quality networking opportunities.
- How to use social media to support your professional networking efforts.

The key for your success

Most successful people will say that networking has played an important role in their careers. I would challenge anyone who claims that his or her success was completely self-determined. No matter what your career, a professional network can be extremely helpful.

Actors, athletes, artists, and musicians, in addition to business people, civil servants, politicians, medical professionals, lawyers, teachers, doctors, and not-for-profit professionals all benefit from the relationships nurtured by a robust professional network.

Professional success in every industry is a team effort. Your team, or your professional network may include people within your own organization, your industry, or related industries. It may also include your business partners, former colleagues, college classmates, and people who belong to the same professional associations.

Developing relationships with people who want to and are able to help you is a worthwhile investment of your time and resources. These are the people who will help when you need it most. This is a long-term investment of your time in building relationships with other people.

> **TIP**
>
> *Professional success in every industry is a team effort. Who is on your team?*

Your professional network will be developed and maintained over your entire career. Actively participate in your network and help others, as you would like others to help you. Maintain these business relationships in good times and bad—while you are fully employed, unemployed, or in between. A strong professional network is as valuable to a first year employee as it is to the CEO. It is as important to someone working in a tech start-up in Silicon Valley as it is to the person teaching elementary school. Developing your own professional network will lead to more success than

> **TIP**
>
> *Developing your own professional network will lead to more success than almost anything else you do in your career.*

almost anything else you do in your career. It is the key to your professional success.

Why networking is important

Like any good investment, the hours you put into active networking will pay off well in your future and the benefits are likely to multiply over time. Some of the many benefits that may be exchanged among people in your professional network include:

- Job opportunities.

- Professional recommendations.

- New customers, clients, investors, advisors.

- New business partners.

- Joint-venture opportunities.

- Recommendations for professional services such as accountants, lawyers, graphic artists, or web developers.

- News, trends, and important events in your industry or business community.

- Referrals to other people who you may want to join your network.

- Recommendations for personal service providers such as doctors, restaurants, vacation spots, and more.

You'll notice that I said above, "the many benefits that may be exchanged among people." I didn't say, "the many benefits that you may receive." A professional network always involves give and take. And give usually comes first.

What is the secret to making networking fun?

Do you dread networking? Does the thought of it make you anxious or uncomfortable?

Do you want to know the one secret to making networking fun? Here it is: Approach networking with an attitude of giving. Focus on how you can help other people.

Everyone has something of value to share. No matter their age, experience level, or current employment status, everyone has something to offer in a networking situation. You have former college classmates, current friends, and neighbors who work in a variety of industries and organizations. Perhaps someone in your network is an entrepreneur, went to graduate school, or worked overseas. I know that at some point in your life, you've visited a doctor, eaten in a restaurant, taken a vacation, or volunteered your time with a not-for-profit or political organization.

These are just a few of the resources that you bring to any networking situation. And none of these resources depend on your age, seniority, or ability to hire. Everyone has something to bring to a networking situation.

> Several years ago, I met a recent graduate at a networking event. At the time, I was almost 20 years older than he. We talked about his interests and my previous experience in the financial services industry—one of the few things we shared in common, at least on the surface. As the conversation progressed and he asked me about my current professional interests, we discovered that I was in the same business as his father and he made an introduction as a follow-up to our meeting. Neither of us could have anticipated this when we met.
>
> Everyone has something to offer in a networking situation—no matter the difference in age or experience.

Networking = building professional relationships

Successful professionals understand that networking is really about building relationships with other people. Although these relationships are professional in nature they are similar to the relationships in your personal life.

Your professional relationships need to be nurtured. Both people need to recognize the benefits of their relationship and contribute to it. Have you ever had a friend or family member who seems to only take from your relationship, but doesn't contribute? Relationships are not in balance at all times, but there must be some degree of equality over the long term or else it is not sustainable. This is as true for professional relationships as it is with personal relationships.

Why does networking get a bad rap?

Some people have a negative reaction to the idea of networking. Others avoid networking opportunities because they are uncomfortable or fearful. If the prospect of networking makes you uneasy, you have the wrong idea of what networking is about.

At a networking event, you may have seen someone grabbing as many business cards as possible while stuffing their card into your hand. Maybe you met someone who talked endlessly about himself or herself while never pausing to allow others to introduce themselves. You may have experienced the pushy follow-up, where someone you didn't want to meet is calling you to sell you something you don't want to buy.

Hopefully, this is not your approach to networking. If it is, immediately stop! You are contributing to the impression that "networking" is a bad word. No one would blame you for being turned off by such behavior. But that is not networking. It is just annoying. Unless a networking group or event is specifically designed for people to sell or pitch each other, such behavior is simply not appropriate in a professional networking situation.

"Networking" is not a bad word, but there are many bad networkers. They are not bad people, but they have never learned the correct way to network. They have not applied the "golden rule of networking."

THE GOLDEN RULE OF NETWORKING

All professional relationships require care and tending. Like a farmer who tends his field, the effective networker should not expect immediate results. Good networking cannot be rushed. Here are some additional points to remember while building your professional network:

- Relationships are fragile and take years to build, but only seconds to destroy. Be mindful of the delicate nature of relationships.

- Do for others as you would like others to do for you.

- If you attend a networking event for the first time and are desperate to find a job, your desperation will making building a relationship difficult.

- Don't expect to take from a group before you have first contributed.

- Other people at a networking event may feel a sense of anxiety. Be the first to smile, shake someone's hand, and introduce yourself.

If you avoid networking situations because you are uncomfortable or fearful, keep reading. Do you attend an occasional networking event, collect a few business cards, and feel like you've done your best? In either case, you're missing the best part. The rest of this chapter will outline the steps for effective networking and reveal the secret that makes networking fun.

NETWORKING TIPS

DO

- Contribute to the networking group.

- Build and maintain person-to-person relationships.

- Help others as much as you can.

- Carefully listen to others in conversation.

DON'T

- Focus only on the personal benefits you expect.

- Pitch or sell to someone immediately upon meeting them.

- Talk more than you listen.

- Ignore the formal or informal rules (or norms) of the group.

How to effectively network

The formula for success in networking is to think of it as a way to build professional relationships. When viewed from this perspective, the idea of networking will take on fresh meaning.

It's natural to be a little uncomfortable when you first begin networking. This section will tell you how to prepare for a networking event, what to do during the event, and how to follow up afterwards. This knowledge along with practice will reduce your anxiety.

Of course, not all networking happens at an official networking event. You can network at a trade show or a convention, on the subway or bus commuting to work, in the lobby of your

TIP

In some cultures, including many Asian cultures, writing on a person's business card is considered an insult.

doctor's office, or in an elevator. This chapter is organized using a networking event as an example, but the information about preparation and follow up applies to formal and informal networking in planned or serendipitous locations.

PREPARE BEFOREHAND

Preparation is the key to mastering most new skills. For networking, a little preparation will go a long way. Anxiety related to networking is often a result of being unsure what to say. Meeting someone in a professional networking situation is no different than meeting a new friend in a social situation. The purpose is to begin to get to know the other person and start to build a relationship. If either person is feeling uncomfortable or awkward, it could be because of trying to take a shortcut—trying to skip over the relationship building part and jump right into a business transaction. Being in such a hurry just doesn't feel right to most people. Think of the difference between jumping into the deep end of a cold pool and easing yourself down the steps until your body adjusts to the temperature. That's how you should approach networking.

You can prepare for any new networking situation by planning and practicing ahead of time. Think through what you will say and practice saying it. When you've prepared and rehearsed, your words will sound natural and the conversation will flow. You and the person with whom you are speaking will both feel more comfortable.

Preparation will take time and effort. Don't wait until you walk in the door to begin preparing. Take an hour with a blank page and put some thought into this work. The investment of time and effort will be rewarded.

The most common question at a networking event is "What do you do?" Since you know the question will be asked prepare your answer. Write two versions of your answer:

- short response—a 20-second or less version (approximately 30-40 words depending on your rate of speech).

- long response—a two-minute version (approximately 200-250 words).

Short Response

The short response of your answer to the question, "What do you do?" should be no more than 20 seconds long. This equates to approximately 30-40 words depending on your rate of speech.

In other books and articles about networking, you may see the term "twenty-second pitch" which is similar to the term I am using here. The idea is similar, but the emphasis is different. If you are pitching or selling in the first 20 seconds you meet someone, then you've missed the point of networking and the importance of building a relationship.

The first 20 seconds are critical. Answer the question, "What do you do?" in such a way that you make a memorable impression in the mind of the person to whom you are responding. Your answer should help move the conversation forward.

"I am a lawyer," you could say or "I am a salesperson," but answers like these don't move the conversation forward or make it easy for the person to remember you. You reveal little about yourself and miss the opportunity to share how you are different from the one million lawyers or tens of millions of salespeople across the country. You make it difficult for the person you are meeting to respond. "That's nice," is about all they can say, or just "oh." If you're lucky and the person you are meeting is in the same profession, you might get "me too" as a response. At this point, the conversation is headed off the rails.

Instead, your short version should add some detail, color, or flavor about the type of lawyer, salesperson, or other professional you are. What is your specialty or expertise? Who are your customers/clients? What about your role is unique? Compare these:

"I am a lawyer" vs. "I advise small to medium-sized corporate clients about employment matters."

"I am a salesperson" vs. "I provide custom security systems to keep my clients and their families, homes, and businesses safe."

The answers that will enhance the conversation are obvious and they will make you more memorable. This part of your short version answer is the "hook"—the details that prompt one or more follow-up questions or comments in response. Your hook should be intriguing enough that it is memorable, it sparks curiosity, and invites further discussion.

With that as guidance, develop your short response by writing several versions of your response. Then continue to refine them. Once you are happy with the words on paper, speak them out loud into a voice recorder. Listen to your recording. Evaluate how it sounds to you. Revise as necessary. Now is also a good time to check the timing, which should be no longer than 20 seconds (ten seconds is better). By now, these words should sound and feel natural to you. If not, find new words.

After you're satisfied with the results, practice out loud with friends or colleagues. Seek their feedback. Continue to practice until your response sounds natural instead of rehearsed.

> **TIP**
>
> *By combining your short and long responses, you have an answer to a classic interview question—"Tell me about yourself." In an interview situation, you'll want to expand on your answer and take full advantage of this opportunity to focus on your skills and accomplishments.*

Long Response

Since your short response to the question, "What do you do?" is interesting and includes an effective hook, the person to whom you are speaking will likely ask the follow-up question. Remember that the hook you include in your short response should prompt a follow-up question or comment. You will likely be able to anticipate the question or comment that you get in response to your hook; you can prepare and hone your long response.

Sometimes referred to as a two minute pitch, two minute commercial, or elevator pitch, your long response is meant to provide additional information about what you do. It shows how the person with whom you are speaking might help you. You want to answer the question for the other person.

Continuing with the two examples from above, here is a sample dialogue to consider as you design your own long response.

The lawyer's short response was:

> I advise small to medium-sized corporate clients regarding employment matters.

Here is what the lawyer's long response might sound like:

> Our firm has been established for 50 years and we have more than 150 lawyers in our offices in New York and Connecticut. The firm has several Fortune 500 clients, but we focus on smaller firms who don't usually maintain in-house counsel with the expertise our firm provides. We specialize in employment law and labor relations. Recently, the three managing partners of our firm were all named to the "Top 100 Lawyer" list.

If you met this lawyer at a networking event, what do you know after listening to their short and long responses? First, you know from the lawyer's short response—"I advise small to medium-sized corporate clients regarding employment matters."—that the lawyer would welcome an introduction to someone in your network who works for a small to medium-size corporation. From the lawyer's long response, you also know the specific area of legal expertise—employment law.

Next, you know that a potential client for this lawyer would likely be based in New York or Connecticut, since law firms practice within state boundaries. You also know that this law firm is well established—having been around for more than 50 years and, finally, that the managing partners are well regarded in the legal profession.

With this information, you can mentally scan your own professional network and determine if there is someone who might benefit from an introduction to this lawyer. Perhaps your own organization needs this type of expertise or you have a friend who is currently negotiating his own employment contract and needs legal advice. If you can't think of anyone who might need this lawyer's services immediately, you could consider an introduction to someone else in your network who might have a direct connection.

The sales person's short response is:

> I provide custom security systems to keep my clients and their families, homes, and businesses safe.

Here is what the sales person's long response might sound like:

> I have been in the security industry for more than 30 years. After ten years as a police officer, I transitioned into the private sector and joined the top security systems company as a technician. After several years installing these systems, I joined the company's sales team and worked my way up the ranks. Today, I run their West Coast division and am responsible for 200 sales people and 35 percent of the company's revenue. The firm specializes in commercial systems, but our technology also adapts to residential applications—especially multi-unit dwellings such as apartments, condos, and hotels.

If you met this sales person at a networking event, what do you know after listening to his or her short and long responses? First, you know that this person is highly knowledgeable about security with a background in law enforcement and 20 years of experience installing and selling security systems.

Next, you know that this person is well established in his or her organization, having started as a technician and worked their way to a senior management position with major personnel and revenue responsibility. You also know that it's likely that the company covers most of the United States. Finally, you know that their primary customers are commercial, but include residential as well.

With such information, you can scan your own professional network for potential customers for this sales person. If you can't think of anyone with an immediate need for a security system, is there someone in your network who might benefit by an introduction to this person? Maybe you know a real estate developer who would consider installing security systems in the houses he builds. Or perhaps you know someone in the insurance industry who deals with claims as a result of theft or burglary.

Lessons from networking conversation examples

These are highly simplified examples, but they do emphasize several key points. First, in my experience, 99 percent of networking situations begin with "What do you do?" You will be ready to answer effectively if you've prepared and practiced a short response that includes a hook and you have a well thought out long response. Is your hook eliciting the follow-up question or comment you intend? If not, consider changing it. It's impossible to predict with certainty how people will respond, but being prepared will enable you to modify your answers as necessary.

Second, because you are prepared for the opening part of the networking conversation, the rest will probably flow smoothly. The result: better outcomes in relationship building. There is a lot more to establishing and maintaining a professional network than an introductory conversation. Of course, your responses will change as your career develops. Your responses also may vary with your goals for a particular networking situation.

Third, professional networking is not about a transaction (getting a job, making a sale, acquiring a client, investor, etc.). Instead it is about building a mutually beneficial relationship in which the mutual benefit accrues over time. The examples here focus only on one side of the conversation. Your preparation and approach to the networking conversation might help guide the person to whom you are speaking if they are less well prepared or less comfortable.

Finally, always enter a networking event or situation with the mindset of what you can do to help someone else. As you are looking for these opportunities, you can help others help you by clearly describing what you do and whom you'd like to meet.

AT THE EVENT – YOU'RE ON!

For people nervous about networking, showing up to a networking event may be the biggest hurdle of all. I hope that by preparing for that inevitable question, "What do you do?" you feel more confident and less anxious. If not, spend more time practicing and rehearsing your short and long responses. Practice your dialogue with a voice recorder, video recorder, or a friend.

The moment has arrived. You are attending a networking event or will be in a situation where you know networking will occur.

Arrive early

If you're attending an event at which you don't know many people, arrive early. Unlike being fashionably late to a social function, arriving early at a networking event makes it easier to become part of the party instead of feeling like you've arrived at a party that has started without you.

Meet the event organizer or host

Another benefit to arriving early is that you often will have a chance to meet the person who organized or is hosting the event. This is a good person to know. If you are new to the particular group or event, you can mention this to the host and ask to be introduced to specific people. For example, you might say: "I am an accountant and would be very interested in meeting small business owners." Or, "I am trying to meet someone who works with XYZ Company. Do you know if anyone from that company will be at this event?"

Remember, the key to networking is helping other people. If you ask for an introduction, it is important to offer your assistance. You may say, "As an accountant, I am able to refer people to financial advisors, so if there is anyone here who is looking for a financial advisor, I would be happy to make the introduction." Or say, "As an accountant, I offer a free 30-minute consultation to non-profit firms on how to run their bookkeeping. If there are any nonprofit organizations represented at this event, I would be happy to speak with them." By doing this, you have also helped the organizer create a win-win-win situation for others attending.

Also, if you meet one of the event's organizers, volunteer to help plan the next networking event or spread the word through a social media campaign. By helping to plan an event, you'll naturally meet other people and build your network at the same time.

Work the room – location matters

Where you stand in the room at a networking event can change the outcome for you. The two most important locations are the registration table and the beverage table.

If the event you're attending has a registration table, this is where it all begins. Say hello to the person behind you in line. Linger after you've registered and received your nametag. This is a great place to strike up a conversation as people first arrive. Examine the nametags for people you'd like to meet and ask the organizers to introduce you when the person arrives.

NAMETAGS DON'T DESERVE MUCH THOUGHT, RIGHT? WRONG!

At a networking event, you will meet people for the first time and you want to give them the maximum opportunity to remember your name. Attach your nametag very high on your right lapel. Do this because you are usually extending your right hand to shake, so that side of your body will also be slightly extended forward. This makes it easier for the person to read your nametag without having to look across your body.

The other key location is the beverage table. Depending on the event, it could be coffee or cocktails. People will often linger after getting a beverage, which is an ideal time to start a conversation. When it is your turn to order a drink from the bartender, turn and offer to get something for the person behind you in line. I've found this location much more effective than a food table. Once people have food on their plate, they are less inclined to pause for a conversation.

Groups of two, three, or more

People standing by themselves at an event will welcome your approach. They've chosen to attend a networking event, so at some level they are interested in meeting other people, but perhaps they are shy or uncomfortable. If you approach them, you get the credit for having the confidence. Be a hero. You both win!

It is easier to approach a group of three or more people rather than just two people. Three or more people standing in a group are usually discussing public matters. Two people might be talking about a private issue. You can also assess the conversation by how close people are to each other. The closer they stand, the less likely they will be receptive to an outsider joining their conversation.

THERE'S AN APP FOR THAT!

Several smartphone apps let you exchange contact information with someone else. ✗ However, before relying on this method, you should consider:

- Will the person you meet have a smart phone with a compatible app?

- What is his or her preferred method to exchange information?

- What will you do if your phone is out of power?

- Is the physical business card exchange ritual important in his or her culture?

Even if you use a smartphone app, take some business cards as well.

What do you do if you approach a group and sense that you've interrupted a private discussion? A simple statement is best. "I hope I didn't interrupt." Or, "I'm sorry if I interrupted your conversation." That will usually suffice. Most people will welcome you into their conversation.

Keep the conversation going

People like to talk about themselves. To keep a conversation naturally flowing, consider asking these questions. Modify them for the person with whom you are speaking and for each unique situation.

- How did you get started in your career or industry?

- How long have you been a (career or profession)? Or, how long have you been with your current organization?

- What do you like most about your job or career?

- What do you find most challenging? Most rewarding?

- How does the current situation (an economic/social/legal/political issue) impact your industry or job?

- What trends are developing in your industry? How does globalization affect your business?

Such questions can sustain a thirty-minute conversation, even with a person who's not particularly talkative.

The simple questions above are appropriate for the first time you meet someone. They are good conversation starters and sustainers. What do you discuss with people you've met before? There are dozens of professional topics and none of them involve the current weather. Seek others' opinions on issues effecting your industry or the economy.

A graceful exit

Once you've met someone and your conversation has run it's natural course, don't hesitate to move on and meet other people. Besides the potentially awkward introductory conversation, this is the next place where I see people struggle during a networking event. There is nothing wrong with saying: "It's been a pleasure meeting you and I hope to see you again." You are not beholden to speak with one person for the entire event. Another way to end a conversation is to make an introduction to someone else in the room.

NETWORKING CHECKLIST

Before attending a networking event ask yourself:

- Am I going with the mindset to help others?

- Have I prepared and practiced my short and long responses?

- Why am I attending this event? What outcome am I seeking?

AFTER THE EVENT – THE FOLLOW-UP

The follow-up to a networking event is the most overlooked aspect, but it is the most important. Without an effective follow-up, you've wasted your time. It shocks me that people will take the time and spend the money involved to attend an event and then not properly follow up with people they meet.

Effective follow-up after meeting someone in a professional networking situation includes:

- Contact people with whom you met to express appreciation for their time. A simple email is sufficient. A hand written note will stand out.

- Provide your contact information if you did not when you initially met.

- Follow through right away with any information, referral, or introduction you may have discussed.

- Decide how you might stay connected with this person. How will you continue to develop this relationship? ✘

- Connect on LinkedIn or another social media channel if appropriate.

Where to find networking opportunities

There are formal networking groups and informal networking opportunities all around. Most people can identify three to five convenient opportunities without much effort. A networking opportunity isn't always labeled as such. Informal networking can happen anywhere. Here are a few suggestions for formal and informal networking opportunities:

Your Company or Organization

More and more, organizations are recognizing the power of networking and the benefits of employees building professional relationships across teams, business units, and divisions. If your organization doesn't have a formal networking program, speak to your manager or the human resources department about starting one.

There may be a group of first-year hires that would benefit from knowing each other and learning more about the organization. Another scenario might involve employees from one office networking with colleagues in another office or physical location. If your organization includes people who work remotely or

> **TIP**
>
> *LinkedIn is a tool for networking, but not a substitute. It allows you to stay informed about what your network is doing and easily contribute leads, information, support, and other information.* ✖

are frequently on the road visiting customers or clients (such as sales people or consultants), there is most certainly a benefit in getting together in person. It's great to have occasions when everyone gathers in the same place to build and strengthen professional relationships. If your organization is small and everyone knows one another, there may be benefit in networking with another company or organization in a related industry.

Trade and Professional Associations

Industry-focused trade groups and professional associations are good places to find networking events. For many of these associations, hosting networking events is a benefit it provides to its members. Many of these organizations have local, regional, national and/or international chapters. Find out if there are networking events in your geographic area and, if not, contact the association's leadership and offer to organize and host an event.

Your alumni association

Your college or university alumni group may offer formal or informal opportunities for networking. Your fellow alumni may represent a diverse set of occupations, industries, and professions that can greatly expand your own professional network.

Your hobbies and interests

Do you belong to a runner's club, a country club, or a book club? Such organizations are great places for informal networking. Although you don't want to hijack these groups for your own purposes, they provide ideal opportunities to build relationships with people who may have related business interests and/or share personal interests.

Local business and civic groups

Every community has an array of local networking opportunities. Even small communities have chambers of commerce or similar local groups that offer networking opportunities.

Professional networking organizations

There are professional networking groups focused on sharing referrals and business leads. Some of these groups measure their success in terms of dollars transacted. These types of events can be enormously valuable for certain industries and professionals. ⚒

Meetup.com

With almost 20 million members and 180,000 groups around the globe, Meetup.com is a great source for networking events in your community. You may want to vet the group and its organizers to ensure the quality of the event before investing your time. ⚒

Start your own

Consider starting your own networking event. Perhaps your alumni association doesn't have a presence in your geographic region or a professional association to which you belong doesn't have the bandwidth to plan an event in your area.

In designing your own networking group, you may do so outside of a specific organization. Invite people from a single industry, a group of related industries, or a mix of people from a wide variety of industries who are genuinely interested in building their professional networks. As the organizer of this type of event, you benefit by knowing everyone and everyone knowing you. And of course, those you invite must benefit also. ⚒

What makes a high quality networking group or event?

Your time is valuable and you want to choose a high-quality networking group. Here are a few distinguishing factors that usually indicate a high quality group:

• Events or meetings occur regularly (at least quarterly) and are scheduled well ahead of time.

• The group continuously seeks to add new members, topics, or formats.

• Everyone in the group welcomes new attendees.

• There is a clear expectation among members as to the appropriate use of member's contact information.

Social media and professional networking

Facebook, LinkedIn, Twitter, Google+ and other social media platforms are tools for networking, but they are not substitutes. Generally speaking, LinkedIn is considered to be the primary professional networking platform. On this platform, there is not a lot of tolerance for pictures of food or your pet or your pet eating food. Keep it professional.

Networking is about building a professional relationship and you do not build a relationship via social media. You can use these tools to communicate and stay connected between the times when you see someone in person. Nothing, I repeat NOTHING, substitutes for building a professional relationship, person-to-person.

> **TIP**
>
> *Professional relationships are built one-to-one, person-to-person.*

Here are some guidelines for using social media in a career or professional context:

• Use LinkedIn to connect with someone you have met in person. This is a great way to stay connected with your professional network.

- Join LinkedIn Groups that are related to your career, profession, or industry. It may make sense to connect with other individuals in the group.

- It may be appropriate to follow someone on Twitter—especially if they use Twitter professionally. Use your judgment here.

- For many people, Facebook tends to be personal, so don't assume it is OK to "Friend" someone after meeting them at a professional networking event.

- Be cautious about copyright, privacy, and confidentiality when posting on any social media site.

Of course, social media tools can be a tremendous help for staying connected with your current network. Remember that these tools are not substitutes for maintaining relationships in person. Relationship maintenance will take an extra effort from you beyond the ease of scrolling Facebook

> **TIP**
>
> *When sending a "Connect" request on LinkedIn, personalize the message. Don't use the standard message, "I'd like to add you to my professional network." It screams, "I don't know you well enough to write a personal message."*

and Twitter posts each day. You'll want to schedule time on a regular basis to meet face-to-face with the people who make up your professional network.

ACCELERATE YOUR CAREER EXPERIENCE - NEXT STEPS

1. If you don't have a LinkedIn profile, create one now. You can upload your resume to begin your profile. If you do, be sure you've had it reviewed by a professional resume writer (check out the Professional Association of Resume Writers and Career Coaches

at www.parw.com or the National Resume Writers Association at www.thenrwa.com). But remember, LinkedIn is an important tool, but it is not a substitute for one-to-one networking. ✘

2. Participate in at least three networking opportunities in the next three months. These don't have to be formal networking events and could include conferences, happy hours with colleagues, coffee with someone who works in your organization, or lunch with a fellow alumnus who works in your industry.

3. Decide and commit to attend at least one networking event per quarter. One per month is ideal.

4. Practice the skills you've learned in this chapter and the Additional Resources while attending one networking event this month. Follow up as appropriate with the people you met.

5. If you need a little inspiration to take action, read *The Go-Giver.*

ADDITIONAL RESOURCES ✘

The Go-Giver: A Little Story About a Powerful Business Idea
by Bob Burg and John David Mann

Why? This is a superbly written parable whose main message is that in business, as in life, it is better to give than to receive. *The Go-Giver* is both inspirational and aspirational as you build your professional network. I can't recommend it highly enough.

How to Win Friends & Influence People in the Digital Age
by Dale Carnegie & Associates

Why? So much more than about networking, this book is an update of the original classic written by Dale Carnegie in 1936. The original title is often cited as the book that launched the entire self-help genre—currently an $11 billion industry, according to *New York Magazine.*

Million Dollar Networking: The Sure Way to Find, Grow, and Keep Your Business
by Andrea R. Nierenberg

Why? Andrea Nierenberg is a world-renowned business authority with 25 years experience in sales and marketing. Her books taught me a lot about successful networking early in my career.

LinkedIn Official Blog
Why? If you want to learn more about LinkedIn, go right to the source. There are hundreds of blog posts arranged by topic and searchable by keyword.

How to Really use LinkedIn
by Jan Vermeiren

Why? This book is written for a broad audience—from the LinkedIn novice to the advanced user—and includes instruction on using the tool and detailed strategies for creating your profile, building your own professional network, and engaging with groups. You can download a full copy of the book for free and access tools, videos, webinars, and self-assessment tools.

I'm On LinkedIn, Now What? (Third Edition)
by Jason Alba

Why? This book covers the "nuts and bolts" of the LinkedIn platform. Alba's website, JibberJobber is designed as a job search tool that is meant to complement other online social networks. Also, check out the JibberJobber group on LinkedIn.

4

BUSINESS WRITING

It's none of their business that you have to learn to write.
Let them think you were born that way.

ERNEST HEMINGWAY

In this chapter you will learn:

- That written communication can make or break your career.

- Three common forms of business writing and guidelines for each.

- How to practice and improve your business writing so you can showcase your underlying talents and abilities.

Written communication can make or break your career

The importance of your ability to write clearly, concisely, and correctly cannot be emphasized enough. For better or worse, the quality of your written communication will directly reflect on your underlying talent and ability. The better you write, the more competent people will think you are.

Consider this very common scenario: Your supervisor asks you to draft a presentation for an important meeting. It may be to introduce a new product, to analyze your organization's competitors in a new market, or to research a new government policy. This is the first major assignment for which you've been given primary responsibility. Naturally, you are eager to do well and impress your supervisor and colleagues.

You begin with online research. You study data from a recent survey and analyze public documents. You read dozens of relevant news stories. After a full week of collecting and analyzing facts and figures, you are ready to document your research and conclusions in a presentation to your supervisor and colleagues.

While you may have done outstanding research and analyzed vast quantities of data, unless you can produce an equally high quality, written summary of your conclusions, your hard work won't matter. You will be judged based only on the end product, the presentation. And if that presentation is poorly written, all of your research and analysis will fall under the same negative shadow. You cannot escape it. Poor quality written communication in the workplace is a career black hole —a nearly inescapable trap—that can break your career.

When you graduated, you may have felt a sense of relief that term papers and other written assignments were behind you. In fact, many graduates choose careers in accounting, engineering, or computer science because they didn't like classes that required a lot of writing. If you are one of these people I have some bad news. As a professional in any industry, writing is one of the most important skills.

Writing is the primary form of workplace communication. So, if you think you are finished with writing because you are finished with college, think again. The good news is that like the other skills in this book, written communication can be practiced and improved.

Here's more good news. Generally, the average quality of written communication in the workplace is just that—average. With some consistent practice and mastery of a few simple grammar and punctuation rules, the quality of your writing will improve and you'll stand out among your peers.

CHECK YOURSELF – GRAMMAR QUIZ

To evaluate your command of some common grammar and punctuation rules that are found in everyday business writing, identify the errors in the following sentences:

1. She plans to go to the meeting with Ben and I.

2. That is the guy that traveled with us to the convention.

3. Who will you go to the appointment with?

4. She can write as well as me.

5. The manager's presentation caused a chilly affect in the room.

6. The new manual was approved by the CEO.

7. The companys president said that business is profitable.

8. Our business is childrens' literature.

9. There are two reasons to buy the plan now; your health and your age.

10. This is the book where the rule comes from.

Check your answers in the Link Library. ✗ How did you do on the quiz?

High quality writing is a requirement for being a high quality professional. Outstanding writing can help make you an outstanding professional. You gain a competitive advantage in your career by improving your writing skills. Improve this skill and your work will be noticed and your efforts rewarded. Here are two scenarios to illustrate the point:

SCENARIO #1:

Your assignment is to document the current process for handling customer service inquiries for your organization and to recommend improvements in a written report. To gather the information you need for this project, you speak with the manager of the customer service department, interview the five most experienced employees of that department. In addition, you review over one hundred complaints that the department received about poor customer service responses, and study a white paper written by your industry trade association entitled *Best Practices in Customer Service.*

After you've collected the data, underlined dozens of key facts and statistics and analyzed the research, you are ready to write the report. Now imagine this—you've broken your arm and are not able to compile the report yourself. Your manager arranges for you to collaborate with a colleague. Would you rather collaborate with your colleague, Bill, who majored in English or your colleague, Kimberly, who was a math major? Even though the underlying work, including your data and research is the same, which team—you and the English major or you and the math major—will likely produce a higher quality, written report?

SCENARIO #2:

You and your co-worker are given similar assignments—analyze and then write a report about the products offered by your company's top competitors in the marketplace.

You research the available products, read online customer reviews, study media reports, and analyze all other publically-available information you can find. You spend over 40 hours on research and analysis. By your estimate, your co-worker has spent about half that amount of time. While you were skipping lunch and eating dinner at your desk, he was taking long lunches and leaving the office at 5 p.m. every day.

The deadline arrives and you each submit your written reports. Your report is ten pages long and includes twelve graphs. Unfortunately, it also includes two typos and a few grammatical errors.

Your colleague writes a five-page report with three key graphs, an executive summary, and no typos or grammatical errors.

Which report will be more favorably judged? What assumptions will people make about the quality of the research that went into writing each report? What will people assume (rightly or wrongly) about the underlying skills of the person who wrote each report?

During the course of a single year, you could be called upon to write many reports, dozens of presentations, and thousands of emails, letters, and other correspondence. It's not hard to see that if your written communication regularly contains grammatical errors and punctuation mistakes, is excessively wordy, or fails to effectively communicate the main idea, your performance appraisals will be negatively impacted.

A lasting impression

Your written communication will leave a lasting impression. Emails are read, then re-read, and forwarded. Mistakes in grammar, punctuation, and spelling will leave a negative impression among your co-workers, bosses, and clients. In some ways, written communication is more hazardous than verbal communication because it leaves behind a trail of evidence and may cement a negative impression of you.

> **TIP**
>
> *There are a few online grammar-checking tools available. Grammarly.com is one of the leaders in this space.*

Although it's also important to be grammatically correct in your verbal communications, your written words will remind people that either you're a good writer or you are not. Your writing is a lasting record that can be distributed widely and will serve as a constant reminder of your ability (or lack of ability). The quality of your writing will reflect on your job performance. Now that you are convinced that writing can make or break your career, keep reading to learn how to master this very important skill.

TIP

Assume that someone in your organization will read everything you write at work—instant messages, text messages, emails, and documents. This happens more often than you might realize.

Before you send that email with the inappropriate joke or text your colleague about how much you dislike your boss, ask yourself, "Is this message worth my job?"

Common forms of business writing

For simplicity, I've organized business writing into three distinct forms and will provide guidelines for each. The three forms are:

- Short-form (text, IM, Tweet, Facebook, or other social media post).

- Medium-form writing such as emails, memos, and letters.

- Long-form writing such as reports, marketing collateral, documentation, and presentations.

GUIDELINES FOR SHORT-FORM COMMUNICATION

In the business world, short-messaging systems (SMS) such as texting and tweeting are a newly acceptable form of written communication in many organizations. Sometimes limited to only 140 characters (in the case of Twitter), these short message systems require that your writing be succinct and easy to read. Since much of this technology is relatively new, you may know more than your managers and older colleagues about these communications tools.

Texts and instant messaging

As a new professional, don't assume that your manager will communicate with you in the same way that you've been communicating with your classmates and friends. Ask your manager and colleagues about their preferences for text messaging or using another type of instant messaging system, such as Google and Facebook. Make sure you understand and respect their preferences.

TIP

Recognize that there may be generational differences in how you should communicate in your organization or workplace. As a new professional and native user of these relatively new forms of communication, you need to be sensitive to such generational differences. Avoid making biased assumptions.

There may also be security or privacy issues related to confidential information. Check with your manager about his or her preference for communicating via text, telephone, or an instant messenger program. Be sure you read and understand any formal policies regarding communication when sensitive or confidential information is involved.

Texting and instant messaging are quick forms of communication. They're useful when you need a quick answer or want to make a quick response to a single question. You might IM a colleague to find out if he or she is available for a meeting at a certain time, for example. Texting and IM, though, are not meant for long or complex communications that involve multiple questions or ideas.

Just because you use the same text-messaging tool at work as you did in college doesn't mean you use it in the same way. Broken English, slang, shortcuts, emoticons, and general overuse of the medium are not appropriate in a professional context. Others in the work place may view such informality as being unprofessional, so stay vigilant and LOL on your own time! ;)

TEXTING

Texting may be acceptable when you:

• Want to schedule a meeting or check someone's availability.

• Are asking or answering a simple, single question, especially when only a yes or no answer is required.

• Have an emergency that has kept you from work.

- Will be late for an appointment or meeting.

Don't text when you are:

- Having a long, two-way conversation. You should pick up the phone or talk face-to-face.
- Writing long, complex questions or long answers.
- Angry, aggravated, annoyed, or upset—the messages you send could be misunderstood For example, what does it mean if I include this emoticon :(in my text message? Am I sad, upset, angry, or irate?

Social Media

You may be part of a generation known as native users (a.k.a. digital natives) when it comes to social media and online communications. You may have had a Facebook page in high school and tweeted through college. In fact, there's a chance that you have more friends on Facebook and more followers on Twitter than anyone else at the office older than 30. If you are a native user, keep in mind that your supervisor and senior leaders in your organization may not be experienced social media users. They may even regard social media as inappropriate for business use. Ask first and assume nothing before texting or tweeting.

Although there are many ways to use social media, understand that some companies continue to sort through the potential business applications of this technology. Many large organizations and corporations (such as Coca-Cola) and governmental entities (such as the U.S. Centers for Disease Control and Prevention) are already using social media tools that expand far beyond Facebook and Twitter. Many companies have implemented YouTube, Instagram, LinkedIn, Pinterest, Tumblr, or Google+ into their communications plans. They've learned that social media can be good for staying in touch with clients and customers.

Unless using social media is part of your job description, you should not be on Facebook or other social media platforms during the workday. Nor should you tweet personal messages during business hours. In today's world, there are many temptations to connect and communicate with friends. During the workday, though, these are also easy ways to tell your boss that you're not engaged in the work that you were hired to do. If social media is part of your job description, talk to your managers about social media strategy and rules. Read and abide by all company policies regarding social media use.

SOCIAL MEDIA AT WORK – TOP 10 TIPS

1. Keep messages professional—related to your work, your organization, or your industry.

2. Use casual language, but use proper English that is clear and concise.

3. Share news links, trends, and other relevant information.

4. Interact with colleagues, clients, customers, and followers.

5. Avoid slams and unprofessional language.

6. Post only appropriate photos and images. If you are not sure, don't post.

7. AVOID USING ALL CAPS AND EMOTICONS. It can be annoying and look unprofessional.

8. Understand the terms of use for each social media site you use for professional purposes.

9. Find examples from social media experts in your industry and learn from them.

10. Be cautious about sharing information that may be sensitive, confidential, embarrassing, or illegal. Again, if you're not sure, don't post.

Guidelines for medium-form communication

Many of your written communications will be in the form of emails, letters, and memoranda longer than an instant message but shorter than proposals, reports, grant applications, manuals, business plans, and other complex writing. Medium-form writing is generally limited to one or two pages of text.

As with short form writing, any medium length communications should use proper English. Such work should have correct grammar, appropriate punctuation, an awareness of the target audience, and a clear purpose. Treat your first version of a document as a draft. Make it a habit to revise and edit as necessary before hitting the send button. This practice will improve the quality of your writing and protect you from embarrassing mistakes as well.

> **TIP**
>
> *To instantly improve the quality of your writing, write a first draft and set it aside. Review and revise the next day if possible. As you develop this practice you'll teach yourself to write better as you go.*

"I would have written a shorter letter, if I had more time," is a popular saying attributed to various people. That's true. It can take more time to write a brief and to-the-point document than it takes to write a long one. Your reader—be it your boss or your client—will appreciate the brevity. In fact, many people will stop reading a longer than necessary document. A good business practice is to save drafts for an hour. Then go back before sending to see if you can make it shorter.

Here are some general guidelines for writing emails, letters, memos, and any other medium-length communications:

- Follow the guidelines for the short-form communications.

- Grammar matters. Microsoft Word and other word processing programs have basic grammar correction tools, so use them.

- Spelling and punctuation also matter. Spell-check is a standard feature on all word processing software and email systems, so use it. "This isn't important to me," is the message conveyed by frequent typos and misspellings. That's never a signal you want to send.

- Sometimes spell-check programs won't catch discrepancies in simple words such as "to" and "too," so be sure to proofread your work and use a dictionary.

USE EMAIL EFFECTIVELY

When communicating by email, follow these guidelines:

- **Be cautious when using "forward." Does the original sender expect you to forward it? When you send an email, are you sure how it will be handled? Will the recipient forward it to others? Be safe and assume your email will be forwarded.**
- **Be judicious when using "reply all." Does everyone in the thread need to see your response? Or would it be better to reply to the Sender only.**
- **Be careful with the "Bcc" function (blind copy). It can be useful to maintain the privacy of recipients in widely distributed email, but otherwise be cautious.**
- **One method that may improve email efficiency is to say something like this: "I intend to do _______ unless you advise me differently by _________." By explaining your intended next action, you will keep the recipient informed without requiring a response. Some people will appreciate your initiative while others may be uncomfortable with this approach, so check before employing this technique.**

Email dominates your work day

The task of emailing consumes about a fourth of the average worker's day, according to a 2012 report done by the McKinsey Global Institute and International Data Corporation. ⚒ A separate survey estimated that the average corporate email user sends and receives about 105 emails per day.

Despite the many efficiencies of email, the sheer volume means you've got to use this tool effectively or else it can dominate your workday. Consider these issues:

- Emails can be issued at a rapid-fire pace generating multiple responses for a single subject.

- Emails can be distributed to hundreds (or thousands) of people in an instant.

- Email communications have replaced many face-to-face communications. A study done by officebroker.com found that 68 percent of respondents preferred email to face-to-face communication.

- People will read your emails at different times, so the "conversation" can get out of sync. This is especially true when more people are included in the thread. Also, consider the impact of different time zones.

- Many professionals use their email inbox as their "to do" list and/or a project management system despite its inherent weaknesses for this purpose. ✘ Do not use your email inbox as a task management system. It is very inefficient.

Adapt your email style for the workplace

I've been using email for years, you may be thinking, so why do I need to adapt my email style? To be clear, workplace email is NOT the same as personal email. The two are as different as night and day.

For personal email, your language, style, and tone are casual. You may not care about formatting, grammar, or spelling. After all, the worst that can happen is your friends might make fun of you. Professional email carries a much greater downside risk.

How do you adapt your email style? While every company, industry and role will vary, the best way to adapt your style is to match the style of your manager, direct supervisor, and your colleagues—in that order.

First, examine the email styles of your boss and colleagues and tailor your writing to their preferences, observing the frequency with which they send messages and the length of those messages. Then examine the email you receive. Just because someone sends many emails that are short in length, doesn't mean they don't appreciate a single, lengthy email from you. Be receptive to clues that they might provide. Your manager may request a detailed update about a current project, but pay particular attention to any comments about the "novel" that you sent them last time. A comment like that means you might have rambled on too much. Ask for clarification and hone your style to suit your audience.

As ubiquitous as email is, don't allow it to dominate communication with your colleagues, clients, and customers. Allow time for person-to-person discussion. Remember, professional relationships are based on personal interactions. Email will never replace a smile and a friendly handshake.

Avoid email conflict—#@&&@!

If you and a colleague disagree about an issue being discussed via email or if an email exchange has escalated into conflict—stop! Don't click Send!

If you've already exchanged a few emails but the issue remains unresolved and the tension appears to be rising, de-escalate the situation. Meet face-to-face or at least have a phone conversation.

> **TIP**
>
> *Conflict via email usually ends badly for everyone. Resist the temptation to fire back. Instead, be the first to engage in a person-to-person conversation. You will be seen as the hero.* ✕

Disagreements and conflicts can escalate quickly online—

much more quickly than in person. People seem more willing to write something nasty in email (a.k.a. a nasty-gram) than they are to say something nasty in person.

Email and other asynchronous, written communication can easily be misinterpreted. Misinterpretation can arise from a single word. If you are involved in an email communication that is spiraling downward toward full-blown conflict, resist the temptation to fire back by pressing the send button. Instead shift your method of communication.

This approach has several benefits. First, you will be seen as the more emotionally mature and professional person. Second, it will de-escalate the disagreement. Finally, you will more likely uncover the root cause of the disagreement—and, often, that root cause is not what caused the original conflict.

CHECKLIST: MEDIUM-FORM WRITING

Effective emails and memos include:

- No typos or emoticons.

- Proper grammar and spelling. These are even more important than in short form writing.

- A clear subject (or RE: line in the case of a memo or letter).

- A brief summary if it is more than two paragraphs. One sentence or two to three bullets will work.

- A clear purpose, stating a date by which action or a response is required.

- A careful word choice. When composing, assume all electronic communication will not remain private.

GUIDELINES FOR LONG-FORM COMMUNICATION

Long-form writing includes multiple page documents, letters, reports, manuals, grants, proposals, and presentations. All of the guidelines for short and medium-form writing apply here. There are additional guidelines as well.

With long-form documents, you'll want to focus on a clear, well-written summary and/or conclusion. Your document should be organized, formatted, and professional. Use the standards of your organization or industry. The importance of these factors increases as the length of the document increases.

Include a summary at the beginning of the document and a conclusion at the end. The summary at the top of the document, sometimes referred to as an executive summary, provides the reader with a preview of the document. A conclusion at the end of the document will reinforce your key points.

TIP

Using an executive summary and a conclusion for documents greater than three pages, has benefits, including:

• *The document will have more impact on the reader.*

• *The reader is more likely to remember your key points.*

• *Writing the executive summary and conclusion serves as a quality check. It will help you be sure you hit the points you wanted to make.*

The conclusion should not repeat the executive summary word for word. It should restate the points for emphasis.

Your readers will welcome the chance to understand the main ideas of your ten-page report by reading six to eight bullet points. Given the volume of material that all professionals try to read and absorb each day, everyone will welcome an executive summary and conclusion.

Use such enhancements as a table of contents, tables, charts, footnotes, page numbers, and perhaps an index when they would help readers understand your points. All of these functions are available in Microsoft Word. Invest time in learning to use these functions if your job requires you to write long-form documents.

Find examples from your company and industry

Your employer may have standards or examples from which you can work. Your industry may use a specific format or style. For example, a movie script looks a lot different from a legal brief. And a grant application looks different from a marketing report. Find high quality examples of the type of document you are trying to write. Emulate the style, tone, format, length, and even the font of excellent examples.

In addition to a good summary and conclusion, these considerations grow in importance along with the page count:

- Know your potential readers and keep your purpose clear. Focus on the purpose of your document. The marketing department, the sales team, the customer service department, and others within your organization may also read the handbook you create for a new product. Each one of these groups will have a different purpose.

- Decide on the overall appearance or presentation, keeping in mind the impact of your choices on the reader. Your report may be bound, stapled, or inserted into a hardbound notebook. It may have a cover page or a title page. It can be in color or black and white.

- For your core text, consider a type style or font that contributes to the readability of your document. Generally, a font with a serif, such as Times New Roman, is easier to read than a font such as Arial, which has no serifs (san serif). Whatever font you select, be sure that it contributes to the overall professionalism of your report.

BOOKS FOR YOUR DESKTOP (NO, NOT YOUR COMPUTER DESKTOP)

This suggestion is "old school" style. Keeping a few books on your desk will provide you with handy reference tools and it will subtly send the message that you care about the quality of your writing. But only if you use them!

Consider creating a small library that includes:

The Elements of Style by William Strunk and E.B. White is considered to be the bible of writing books. It covers grammar, style, and more. This classic reference has an elegant style of its own.

A style manual. Many businesses designate a consistent company-wide style. Most common are *The Chicago Manual of Style* or the *Associated Press Stylebook and Libel Manual.*

These comprehensive style guides also address usage rules and grammar preferences.

If you don't use the books you'll send the wrong message. Use them or lose them! ⚒

Practice to improve your business writing

Your writing will improve over time if you focus on building this skill. Here's an improvement plan that works:

First, assess your current writing skill level objectively. Study the writing of your colleagues and your supervisor. Read and review the writing of experts in your industry. Include the work of journalists and book authors. You'll get a better idea of standards in your industry. Identify elements in the best writing of others that you can emulate to improve your own writing. Be as objective as you can.

Second, list the differences between your writing and the writing of those whose work you studied. Be specific. Be inclusive. This comparison will help you identify specific areas of improvement for you. You will better understand the ways effective writers make the purpose of their writing clear, express their main ideas clearly, and support their points with solid research. You may realize that you need to concentrate on spelling, punctuation, and grammar. You may discover that others use short, action-oriented sentences while your sentences tend to be long and complicated. You will learn the ways others maintain a flow of ideas while holding the reader's interest, and you'll see how you can too.

Third, customize your findings. Use the specific differences you identified in step two to create a personal writing checklist. Then, methodically utilize your checklist to revise. (And you should always revise). There is no magic to this approach, so use the checklist every time you write a document. Over time, the items on your checklist become habits and your writing will improve. One word of caution here: when you revise you might introduce new errors, so after correcting your most common mistakes, repeat this process.

This approach is guaranteed to improve the quality of your written communication, but only if you use it. This straightforward approach works particularly well for correcting simple punctuation and grammar mistakes, but it will also improve the style and flow of your writing.

SAMPLE WRITING CHECKLIST

Create a list so that you can double-check your weak points. Use your list for everything you write and soon good writing will become a habit.

PURPOSE—What is the purpose of my document? Did I clearly state the main idea, issue, or next steps?

ORGANIZATION – Is the document organized in a way that is understandable to the reader?

GRAMMAR—Have I checked for grammar mistakes?

PUNCTUATION—Is my punctuation correct?

SPELLING—Did I run the spell-check? Am I using any words that the spell-check won't detect?

Too often people spend hours writing a report or a presentation and the main idea isn't clear to readers. What is the purpose of writing the document? Is the goal to get readers to take action, to inform, or to record the details of an event that has occurred?

No matter how strong your skills, always verify the main idea of your writing. Is the primary purpose clear to the reader, easy to find, and properly supported by the rest of the document?

As a final checkpoint, read your work out loud. It can sound different and take on a different meaning. Better yet, have a trusted colleague read it and provide feedback.

Write better by reading more

Read regularly. Read newspapers, magazines, industry journals, white papers, electronic newsletters, and books related to your industry. The more you read, the more you'll become familiar with the style, tone and organization of high-quality writing. What you read serves as a model for your own writing. And, at the same time, you'll be much better informed about your organization and your industry.

Learn, practice, improve, and repeat

I've said it before and I'll say it again. Practice is at the core of accelerating your career experience. You will learn to be a better writer every day through direct observation and practice. But you can accelerate your experience even more by taking a writing course. Nothing is more effective.

If you avoided classes in college that required writing, now is time to sign up for an English composition or business writing class at a local college, an online university, or a MOOC (massive open online course). Most writing classes will help you brush up on grammar and composition—always important for business writing. A writing class also gives you an opportunity to receive feedback, practice, and apply what you learn.

Check your answers on the grammar quiz at the beginning of this chapter. If you scored less than 100 percent, you should be proactively learning to improve your written grammar. A writing class can also be a great benefit here, since it is sometimes difficult to recognize your own grammar mistakes. And, by the way, if you are writing with poor grammar, you are probably also speaking that way.

ACCELERATE YOUR CAREER EXPERIENCE: NEXT STEPS

1. Assess your current skill level. Study the writing practices of your colleagues and superiors. Who writes well? Who doesn't? Note at least three specific improvements you could make.

2. Create your own personalized writing checklist and use it.

3. Identify three industry publications (magazines, journals, white papers, e-newsletters, etc.) and read them regularly. It's common for these publications to be written by professional writers and journalists with knowledge of your industry. As you read, focus on the writing style, tone, and terminology. Emulate the best in your own writing.

4. Take the grammar quiz in this chapter. If you score less than 100 percent, see #3.

5. Purchase and study the books mentioned in the sidebar, *Books for Your Desk,* in this chapter.

6. Enroll in a business writing class at your local college or university, or a MOOC such as Coursera.org or edX.org.

ADDITIONAL RESOURCES ✂

The Elements of Style, Fourth Edition
by William Strunk Jr. and E. B. White

Why? This is the standard reference tool for all English-language writers. Consider keeping a copy in your desk. There is a related online resource at Bartleby.com that allows you to search for rules by key word or browse the full contents of the original 1918 version of this book—all for free.

Woe is I: The Grammarphobe's Guide to Better English in Plain English
by Patricia T. O'Connor

Why? This New York Times best-selling grammar book is an enjoyable read for what can be a dry topic. O'Connor also wrote *Words Fail Me: What Everyone Who Writes Should Know About Writing.*

On Writing Well, 30th Anniversary Edition: The Classic Guide to Writing Nonfiction
by William Zinsser

Why? If you spend a significant amount of your work day writing long-form communications, Zinsser's classic book dives deep into the art of writing nonfiction.

Eats, Shoots & Leaves: The Zero Tolerance Approach to Punctuation
by Lynne Truss

Why? This best-selling book about punctuation entertains while it educates. The English language is complex and punctuation can intentionally (or unintentionally) add meaning to a word. Consider the book's title, *"Eats, Shoots & Leaves"* or an alternative *"Eats Shoots & Leaves"*—not a subtle difference.

10 Steps to Successful Business Writing
by Jack Appleman

Why? This book simplifies the process by providing easy-to-follow steps for writing clearly and succinctly.

American Management Association (AMA)

Why? The AMA is a century-old, non-profit membership organization that offers many courses (in-person and online) on all aspects of business writing. If your organization is a member of the AMA, you may be eligible for a discount. In addition to business writing, the AMA offers a broad range of training courses in such subjects as analytical skills, presentation skills, sales skills, project management, interpersonal skills, and more.

Massively Open Online Courses (MOOCs)

Why? Coursera.org and edX.org are two of the leading MOOCs that offer free courses in business writing and English composition (among hundreds of other subjects). These online, self-study programs have some structure with a syllabus, tests, and specific start and completion dates. They also provide flexibility, though, and are convenient for most busy professionals. MOOCs are a great resource for professional development.

Career-ology Blog

Why? Learn how and when to use a hand written note in a business situation. It can be a powerful tool when used correctly.

5

PUBLIC SPEAKING
AND PRESENTATION SKILLS

Failure to prepare is preparing to fail.

BENJAMIN FRANKLIN

In this chapter, you will learn:

- Why public speaking and presentation skills are critical to your career.

- How to overcome the fear of public speaking.

- Practical tips for delivering a great speech or presentation.

Why public speaking and presentation skills are important

You may be the smartest person in the room, but if you can't speak effectively, no one will know it. Your managers, peers, colleagues, customers, clients, and investors will judge your skills and abilities by the way you speak.

If you are one of those people who are deathly afraid of public speaking, you are not alone. Many studies say that people rank the fear of public speaking higher than the fear of death. Jerry Seinfeld said it best: "At a funeral, the average person would rather be in the casket than giving the eulogy." You may say that it isn't fair or accurate to judge a person's professional abilities by the way they speak in public, but that's the way it is. Many things in the working world aren't fair. Like it or not, you will be judged by the way you speak.

You might hope to avoid public speaking as part of your job. If you chose to be an accountant, software programmer, or investment banker because you believe that as long as your debits and credits balance, your software functions, or your deal closes, you won't have to speak in public. That could not be farther from the truth.

Job function doesn't matter. Your role in an organization doesn't matter. Your ability to express your ideas, thoughts, and opinions verbally will have a great impact on your career. You will still need to sell a product or service to a customer, rally your team to take action, persuade a business partner to adopt your viewpoint, convince an investor to invest, or argue your case before a jury.

I am defining public speaking in the broadest possible sense. It includes speaking to three colleagues in your weekly staff meeting, speaking to a small group during a conference call or video chat, speaking to 30 potential clients in a sales presentation, or addressing a crowd of 300 at an industry conference or trade show. The size of your audience doesn't matter. The same skills are required.

TIP

How you say it is as important as what you say.

Great leaders in business, law, politics, technology, nonprofits, education, government, or healthcare are great public speakers. Think of great leaders from history. How many of your memories about these people involve them delivering a great speech?

In this chapter, I refer to a speech and a presentation interchangeably—the difference being a presentation includes the use of PowerPoint or similar visual tools. A speech refers to a formal speech such as standing on a stage behind a lectern, as well as informal verbal communications such as while seated at a conference table or at your desk and speaking via a video chat.

Where you will use this skill

As a new professional, you will most often exercise your public speaking skills during meetings with co-workers and your boss. A weekly staff meeting, a conference call, or one-on-one conversations with your manager are all public speaking situations. These situations (or opportunities) can have a big impact on your career in both positive and negative ways, depending on your ability to verbally express your ideas. You might not think of these opportunities as speeches, but the same skills apply no matter the size of the audience. Use all of these opportunities to practice this critical skill.

On average, workers spend about a third of their time in meetings. Time spent in meetings usually expands as your level of responsibility increases in an organization. No matter your role in the organization or level of seniority, your ability to present ideas in a clear and concise manner while supported by relevant facts will be an important way to demonstrate your value to an organization.

Poor delivery will undermine your message. All the facts, research, data, and well-structured arguments will not convince anyone to adopt your ideas, purchase your products, support your cause, or give you a promotion if your delivery doesn't measure up. Saying, "like, um, you should give me a promotion because I, like, ya know, I am good at my job" doesn't help your case. In fact, speaking like this will undermine your message. Too many new professionals speak this way. Don't let it be you.

THE GOOD, BAD, AND UGLY OF POWERPOINT

Although Microsoft PowerPoint is a useful tool and the standard for most presentations, its overuse can do more harm than good. Avoid common pitfalls by following these suggestions:

- Use separate slides to emphasize your key points.

- Include no more than two-dozen words per slide.

- Never read directly from your PowerPoint screen. Don't use the words on the screen as a crutch.

- Choose a font large enough for your audience to read without binoculars.

- If you have a lot of details to convey, provide a separate document (printed or electronic) after the presentation.

- Don't overload your PowerPoint presentations with links to videos, cartoons, music, or other graphics. If you include any of these features, thoroughly test the technology and have a solid back-up plan if the internet connection fails.

- If you turn off all the lights, your audience may nod off. Instead, turn off only the lights nearest the screen, so the entire room isn't dark.

Overcoming your fear of public speaking

Overcoming the fear of speaking in public is what makes this skill a game-changer for those who can master it. If you are willing to tread where your colleagues will not and if you are willing to confront your own fears and commit to improving this skill, you will be a much more successful public speaker than your peers.

TIP

Your ability to speak well in front of others will have a significant impact on your career. You should practice expressing your ideas clearly and concisely.

Here is the good news. The bar is not very high when it comes to public speaking and presentation. With some practice, you can be better than most of your peers and colleagues. The better your public speaking skills, the more people will assume you know. Unfortunately the opposite is also true.

Weak verbal communication skills will reflect negatively on you.

Does the mere thought of speaking in front of a group cause sweaty palms, a dry mouth, and shaky hands. It does for many people. While this is the body's natural response to anxiety, it is misplaced when it comes to public speaking. After all, you are not going to be eaten by a dinosaur or scorched by a dragon. Nonetheless, the anxiety is real and needs to be addressed.

So how do you overcome a fear of public speaking? There is a simple answer, but again, don't confuse a simple answer with an easy solution. The simple answer is practice. With dedicated and focused practice, you will become a better public speaker. Practice is not always easy and the level of practice required to master the skill of public speaking requires dedication and discipline, but it is achievable. While the answer is simple, the solution may not be easy.

> **TIP**
>
> *Practice is to public speaking as oxygen is to life; without the first, you will surely perish.*

The Proof

Many of you probably think that my simple answer doesn't apply to you. You're too fearful. You've never taken a public speaking class. You're too shy. You're going to get by in your career without having to speak in front of others. Before you dismiss my proposal, consider the following exercise. For ten minutes, speak about your hometown to a group of twenty-five people.

This exercise is not too difficult, right? I am certain that you could do this exercise with very little preparation and only a minimal level of anxiety, if any. Why? One simple reason—you know the subject matter. And this is where practice comes into play in mastering public speaking and presentation skills. Knowing your subject matter as well as you know your hometown is more powerful than any level of anxiety you may face.

In doing this exercise, you might spend a few minutes organizing your thoughts to ensure you are covering all the important points. You would probably not need any notes, and while you might be a little anxious to speak in front of an unfamiliar group, you probably wouldn't describe the exercise as nerve-wracking or fear-inducing. You certainly wouldn't rank this public speaking exercise as something worse than death!

When you are deeply familiar with the topic, your anxiety level will be low. The goal of practice is to become as familiar and comfortable with the topic as you are with the subject of your hometown. When you achieve that level of familiarity, your fear of speaking in front of others will disappear.

I'm going to repeat that point. Become intimately familiar with the subject and content of your speech. Make the words your own words and your anxiety will all but disappear.

TIP

Practice ↑ *= Anxiety* ↓ *= Confidence* ↑ *= Performance* ↑

With practice, your anxiety will be lower resulting in more confidence and a better performance. There is one simple answer for overcoming your fear of public speaking—PRACTICE!

PRIMARY COMPONENTS OF A SPEECH OR PRESENTATION

Now that you know the simple answer for overcoming the fear of public speaking is practice, let's examine the three primary components of a speech or presentation.

1. Purpose—Why are you speaking?
2. Content—What do you want to say?
3. Delivery—How will you say it?

An exceptional speech or presentation is a combination of establishing a clear purpose, creating compelling content, and delivering with confidence. This holds true if you are delivering a two minute or two hour speech.

TIP

> *Outstanding speech or presentation =*
> *Clear Purpose + Compelling Content + Confident Delivery*

PURPOSE—WHY ARE YOU SPEAKING?

To define your purpose, ask yourself three questions. What do you want your audience to do as a result of your speech or presentation? What is the desired outcome? Why should your audience listen or care about your message?

A speech or presentation may fail before it starts if its purpose is unclear. Before you write a single word of content, define the purpose. Don't just think about the purpose, write it down and refer back to it, especially before finalizing the content or beginning to practice the delivery.

Here are some examples of outcomes or objectives for a speech or presentation:

- Build support among colleagues to accept your proposal.

- Convince a customer to purchase your products.

- Persuade a prospective client to sign a contract.

- Sway an undecided voter.

- Explain your reasons for a proposed policy or law.

- Teach students a new topic or subject.

- Provide entertainment, motivation, or inspiration to your team.

Finally, understand that your audience also has a purpose or an intended goal for listening to your speech or presentation. It is easy to assume that your purpose and your audience's purpose are the same. Such an assumption could be a costly mistake.

Let's say you are giving a speech to a group of constituents about a policy change you've proposed. Is the purpose of your speech to rally additional support, educate, or persuade? Will your audience support or challenge the proposed policy? If you are not certain of your audience's purpose, prepare to answer tough questions and rebut any criticism that you may hear.

Here is another common scenario: you are making a sales presentation to a group of prospective customers. Are you selling to an existing customer or are you attempting to win over your competitor's top customer? In the latter case, the customer may be more reluctant to switch and require a different approach.

> **TIP**
>
> *Words have power and well-spoken words have a lot of power.*

The sales presentation that you deliver might include many of the same facts and figures, but the delivery could vary. Knowing your purpose and your audience's goals before the presentation allows you to refine your message and anticipate questions or challenges that may arise.

Understanding the purpose of your speech from the viewpoints of both your audience and yourself will help you determine both the content of your speech and the way you deliver it. As you think about a speech or a presentation, write down the intended purpose. This is also a great way to check that you haven't included extraneous content. After you have finalized the content, revisit your written purpose. And, revisit it again after you have started practicing your delivery.

> **TIP**
>
> *Too many words turn a good speech or presentation bad.*

CONTENT—WHAT DO YOU WANT TO SAY?

When writing a speech or presentation, you should begin with a logical outline like you would with any other written communication. This includes an overview of the points you will cover, the main body, and a conclusion. The conclusion reviews your key points and reinforces your purpose. If your primary purpose is a call to action—vote for my candidate, buy my product, agree with my viewpoint, sign an agreement, or invest in my company—

make sure it is clear.

It is important to provide your audience with a mental road map of what you are going to say. In a written document or a PowerPoint presentation, you can easily and clearly make reference to your outline so the audience doesn't get lost. In a speech, it's especially important to include references as to where you are and where you are going.

Once you're satisfied with your outline, develop the content that supports the main points. Be sure to keep a list of all sources you use in case you need to refer to them later. As you collect content, it is easy to drift off your main point. This can happen when you are trying to add images that increase the visual appeal of a visual aid or presentation slide. To stay on topic as you develop your speech or presentation, ask yourself this key question: Does this content (image, words, etc.) reinforce my message and purpose?

> **TIP**
>
> *A person's average speaking rate is approximately 120 to 150 words per minute. Determine your own speaking rate, so you know how much content to develop given the amount of time you have to speak.*

It is vital to keep within the prescribed time limits for your speech or presentation. Know your rate of speech and take into account that you might speak faster than normal if you are nervous. Knowing your average rate of speech and the prescribed time limits, you can determine how much content to develop.

Read a draft of your speech into a voice recorder so that you can listen to how it sounds. A well-written speech isn't necessarily a well-spoken speech. Just because your content reads well in your mind doesn't mean it will sound good when spoken out loud. You may find that you've chosen words that are difficult to pronounce or cause you to stumble. Reword these parts.

There will usually be several places where a pause will help you emphasize a key point or idea. The pause will also allow space for you to breathe and the audience to think about and absorb what you just said. Words have power, but so does silence.

Once you've developed the content and are confident in the way it sounds when spoken aloud, commit the content to memory. This is where practice makes a big difference.

> **TIP**
>
> The iPhone and other smartphones have good apps for practicing a speech or presentation, including Voice Recorder, Voice Record Pro, and Audio Memos Free.

As I've already discussed, the more familiar you are with the content of your presentation the lower your level of anxiety. Everyone has his or her own techniques for memorization. Whatever method you choose, become as familiar with your speech content as you are with the details of you hometown as in the earlier example. I encourage you to convert your written content into notes that you can use while speaking. The outline you created can serve as a good set of notes. Your notes might also include detailed data or statistics that you will quote. Don't use the full content for your speaker's notes, as this can easily become a crutch and it will be too easy to just read your speech word-for-word.

> **TIP**
>
> Write the word, "pause" in your speech or presentation notes where you want to slow your speech for a dramatic effect. This will serve as a reminder for you. Be comfortable with the silence.

In addition to reducing the level of anxiety, committing your speech or presentation to memory makes you appear more authentic and thereby your message sounds more credible. Your authenticity and credibility will reinforce your purpose. Two people can deliver the same content and the audience will judge those speeches differently based on their perception of the speaker's authenticity and credibility. This is one of the key differences between an average public speaker and a great public speaker. And great public speakers practice so they sound credible.

DELIVERY—HOW WILL YOU SAY IT?

You've written a great speech or presentation and committed your message to memory so that you can speak to you audience in an authentic and credible way. Now you are ready to focus on your delivery. There are many components of delivering a great speech. Here are two key components to consider—your voice and your body language.

Your Voice

The human voice is a complex instrument. Unless you become a professional speaker, you probably don't need to understand all of the complexities, but a general understanding will greatly enhance your delivery.

Volume – Are you speaking loudly enough so that everyone can hear? Are you able to project your voice without straining it? Are you comfortable using a microphone?

Pitch – Are you using your voice's pitch (high or low) to emphasize important points? Do you end statements with a high pitch that makes it sound like a question?

Rate - Do you vary your rate of speech to keep the audience's attention? Does your rate of speech help the audience's ability to comprehend your message?

Enunciation – Are you speaking your words clearly enough that everyone understands?

Practice with some of these vocal effects while you are memorizing your content. While it may be unnatural at first, it will become second nature as you do more public speaking and greatly enhance your delivery.

> **TIP**
>
> *Most professional speakers use vocal exercises to warm up their voices beforehand. There are many techniques you can use, so find one you like and try it. You don't need to be a professional speaker to benefit from these exercises.* ✕

Your Body Language

What is your body language communicating when you speak? If you don't know, you'd better find out because your audience will certainly be aware.

Non-verbal communication is sometimes more important than your content. In fact, some researchers say that 55 percent of communication is body movement, 38 percent is your tone of voice, and only seven percent is your words, according to the frequently cited original research by Professor Ray L. Birdwhistell. ✕

Focus on these four aspects of your body language: your face, your eyes, your hands, and your feet. What is each part of your body saying? Are your hands delivering the same message as your words at that moment? Does your eye contact portray trust and confidence? Does your body language enhance your main message?

Your Face

Your face should be relaxed and you should smile as much as possible. A smile on your face conveys confidence and, after all, that is the image you are trying to project. Most important, the muscles in your face can hold a lot of tension if you are nervous or anxious. Smiling will make you aware of any tension in your face and may help you relax and ease your anxiety.

Your Eyes

Making eye contact with your audience is critical. Even though this can be intimidating for some speakers, you should practice until you are comfortable. Condition yourself to look people directly in their eyes. One way to practice when rehearsing your speech is to visualize yourself looking into the eyes of the people in the audience. It takes some practice, but visualization is a proven technique with many applications.

While you are delivering your speech or presentation, you may find people in the audience who are nodding their heads in affirmation. These are great people to revisit with your eyes often as you look around the room. There is nothing better than this type of positive feedback while you are speaking. There will be others whose eyes you might want to avoid—perhaps those focused on their smart phone or worse, those who are nodding off. It happens to even the best speakers. Avoid looking at these people.

> **TIP**
>
> *There is an old bit of advice out there that says a speaker who is nervous about looking people in the eyes should focus on the foreheads of the people in the audience. That might work with a large audience, but in a smaller room, I can usually tell when a speaker is doing this. I find it distracting. You want to connect with your audience by establishing direct eye contact.*

Your Hands

Many people don't think about this, but your hands are an important part of your speech or presentation. Some people use their hands more that others, but everyone has their own set of natural hand gestures. Understand exactly what your hands are doing to make sure your gestures are in synch with your message. Sometimes this may require developing a new set of gestures and practicing them until they become second nature.

HAND-Y TIPS

Your hands can say a lot when you're delivering a presentation or speech. Here is some advice:

- Keep your hands relaxed at the sides of your body when you are not intentionally gesturing.

- Avoid putting your hands in your pockets.

- Don't repeat the same gesture too often, as it may become a distraction for the listeners.

- Use meaningful gestures to punctuate points in your speech. For example, use your fingers as you elaborate on the first, second, and third points of your speech.

Your Feet

Finally, your feet are an important source of non-verbal communications. This sounds preposterous, right? While standing, your feet largely determine what your body does. Your feet should be planted firmly on the ground. While standing on a podium, stage, or in front of a large room, your feet are likely visible to your audience. Only move your feet in a purposeful way.

For those who have almost conquered the fear of public speaking, the feet are often the last telltale sign of nervousness. If a speaker seems cool, calm, and collected, check his or her feet. A nervous speaker who releases stress through his feet will pace, sway, tap a toe or heel, or stand flat on one foot and lean on the lectern while the other foot sways. Remember to keep both feet flat on the ground.

How do you understand what your hands and feet are doing while you speak? Consider asking someone to watch and record these movements. A Toastmasters club is an excellent way to get this type of feedback.

> **TIP**
>
> *A speaker stands on a podium and places his or her notes on a lectern. Many people mistakenly use the word "podium" when referring to a "lectern." Skilled speakers know the difference.* ✂

TOASTMASTERS INTERNATIONAL

When it comes to mastering public speaking, there is no greater resource than Toastmasters International.

Toastmasters International offers its members a venue for practicing communication and leadership skills. Clubs meet regularly and members fulfill different roles at each meeting. There is a proven curriculum of increasingly more challenging topics, techniques, and formats. Fellow club members evaluate speeches for each other. They also give support and encouragement to speakers of all abilities. Toastmasters International has grown to 14,650 clubs in 126 countries since its founding in 1924.

I encourage you to join Toastmasters. Each club has its own personality, so visit several clubs to find the one that best suits you. Visit the Toastmasters International website to find a club near you. ✗

The use of a video camera is invaluable while practicing public speaking. There is nothing like seeing yourself in action. This method is far superior to someone telling you what you did or did not do. You can use your smart phone or video camera to record yourself. I encourage you to upload the video to your computer so that you can observe the details of your movements on a large screen. This is the single most important tool for self-improvement and mastering the skill of public speaking.

You may not want to upload these videos to YouTube or Facebook for the public to view, but it is helpful to archive your practice videos for a couple of reasons. First, by keeping a historical record of these performances, you will be able to gauge your progress

TIP

Use a video camera to record and then critique yourself while watching on your computer screen.

over time, which will greatly boost your confidence. Second, by keeping a record of past speeches, you can look at your specific habits, such as hand gestures.

PRACTICE YOUR DELIVERY

Here are some other ways that you can improve your delivery:

- Practice a full-length speech using a video recorder at least ten to twenty times. How many times should you practice? The answer is simple: As many times as it takes to master your content.

- Ask someone to count the "ums," "ahs," and "likes" you use. These are filler words and they can kill a good speech. Be comfortable with the sound of silence. Or, use a video/voice recorder and count the filler words. You may be surprised.

- Visualize your audience and the room in which you will deliver your speech.

- Prepare for possible interruptions and distractions such as a ringing cell phone, a microphone or PowerPoint failure, or people who arrive after you've started.

The Day of Your Speech

Finally, the day for delivering your presentation or speech has arrived. You've clearly defined your purpose, developed great content, and refined your delivery. There are still some things you can do to help your speech go well.

If possible, arrive early and get comfortable in the environment, whether it's a conference room or an auditorium. Test all technology, including sound and video equipment. Consider the temperature of the room. If you can adjust it, you'll probably want it cooler than normal.

The seating arrangement of the room can also affect your speech. It is almost certain that at least a few people will arrive late. Reserve several seats near the entrance so latecomers can be seated without distracting you or the other members of the audience.

> ### TIP
>
> *Oops. Your microphone is still on!*
>
> *Celebrities and politicians aren't the only people who may mistakenly assume the microphone is off. It happens to all of us. Once after giving a presentation to a few hundred financial market regulators in Europe, I walked out of the room wearing the live microphone. Luckily, I did not say anything that might have offended the audience. I'll never forget the event host urgently calling after me in his German accent, "Remember, the mic is still on!"*

Finally, get yourself organized at the lectern. Decide where you will keep your notes, a clicker for the projector, and your water. Determine what you will use to keep track of your timing and have that device in clear sight.

ACCELERATE YOUR CAREER EXPERIENCE - NEXT STEPS

1. Join a Toastmasters Club. It is the best way to become a great speaker. Visitors are welcomed in all public clubs. I encourage you to visit several clubs until you find the one you like.

2. Really tune in and critique the speeches you hear in person and on television. What makes them great? What can you learn and apply to your next speech or presentation? What did the speaker do well? What didn't they do well?

3. Learn how to use Prezi.com. Use this new tool instead of PowerPoint during your next presentation and impress your audience.

4. Take every opportunity you can to speak in public. Even your

two-minute update at the next staff meeting is an opportunity to practice this important skill.

5. Identify and use opportunities to practice public speaking and presentation skills at work, in a volunteer organization, at your place of worship, at civic organizations, etc.

ADDITIONAL RESOURCES ✗

Toastmasters International

Why? Toastmasters is the single best resource for one of the most challenging professional skills to acquire and practice. With more than 300,000 members in 14,650 local clubs throughout 126 countries, Toastmasters provides its members with regular, hands-on workshops to improve their speaking skills. All new members follow a well-structured program that covers all aspects of public speaking. After that, members can specialize in dozens of specific speech types. Every Toastmasters club is different, so visit several until you find the right fit. At a cost of less than one hundred dollars per year, Toastmasters is the greatest, most cost-effective resource available.

Clear and to the Point: 8 Psychological Principles for Compelling PowerPoint Presentations
by Stephen M. Kosslyn

Why? Kosslyn is a renowned cognitive neuroscientist and professor of psychology at Harvard University. This book provides eight simple principles for designing a presentation based upon the human perception, memory, and cognition. While rooted in science, this book provides practical advice. It includes hundreds of images and sample slides that illustrate the principles. If you use PowerPoint as a regular part of your job, you MUST read this book.

Speaking Mastery—The Keys to Delivering High Impact Presentations
by David and Michael Hutchison

Why? This book offers real world advice for delivering high impact speeches or presentations. *Speaking Mastery* covers how to deliver your message, develop your content, and build the "internal muscles" to be a great public speaker.

TED.com

Why? TED Talks will inspire, teach, shock, fascinate, amaze, and impress you. There are over 1,900 videos (averaging approximately 18 minutes each) of some of the best public speakers in the world. Watch, learn, and prepare to be amazed.

Prezi.com Blog

Why? The Prezi Blog includes information about using their presentation tool, an incredible and long overdue alternative to PowerPoint. It also has great general presentation tips.

Dale Carnegie Training

Why? Dale Carnegie is considered by many to be the godfather of the entire self-help genre and is famous for the 1936 best selling book, *How to Win Friends and Influence People*—still popular today. Dale Carnegie Training offers online learning and in-person courses and seminars on public speaking and presentations, as well as leadership, sales, negotiations, and management. Check out the website's Resources page for free eBooks, Smartphone Apps and E-Newsletter.

The Presentation Secrets of Steve Jobs: How to Be Insanely Great in Front of Any Audience
by Carmine Gallo

Why? Steve Jobs' presentations are legendary. When thinking about Jobs, most people picture him in a black turtleneck on stage for the latest Apple product launch. In his book, Gallo deconstructs the techniques that Jobs used so masterfully. If you want to raise your game, check out Gallo's other book, Talk Like TED: The 9 Public-speaking secrets of the World's Top Minds.

Speak Up! An Illustrated Guide to Public Speaking
by Douglas M. Fraleigh and Joseph S. Tuman

Why? Speak Up! is an illustrated college-level text book. It also covers issues related to delivering speeches and presentations via modern technology including virtual meetings, vlogs, etc. The paperback version is over 700 pages, so this resource requires a serious commitment.

6

SALES AND NEGOTIATION SKILLS

We are all in sales now.

DANIEL PINK

*In business as in life, you don't get what
you deserve, you get what you negotiate.*

CHESTER L. KARRASS, PH.D.

In this chapter, you will learn:

- There are many similarities between sales skills and negotiation skills.

- Sales and negotiation skills are important for every professional in every type of organization.

- Sales and negotiation skills can be learned and practiced.

- The importance of developing client/customer awareness.

Sales skills and negotiation skills will be discussed interchangeably in this chapter. In order to convey the most important information in a single chapter, I am treating sales and negotiation as a single topic. This is an enormous simplification of these two vast and complex topics. To illustrate this point, Amazon.com has over 500,000 books on "sales" and 25,000 books on "negotiations." There is no possible way to teach either skill in an entire book, let alone a single chapter. The goal is to provide an overview and show you how important sales and negotiation skills are to your career.

Sales vs. negotiations

Sales and negotiations are not individual skills, but instead a complex combination of skills and knowledge including: psychology, politics, economics, communications, relationship building, and strategic thinking. For example, your knowledge of human psychology will help you understand your customer's needs and concerns when trying to sell her a $50,000 consulting engagement. The same skills will also apply when you are negotiating a promotion. Good negotiators usually are also good sales people and vice versa.

Everyone is in sales (Yes, EVERYONE!)

"Who is currently in or will be in a sales role for their company or organization?" is a question I often ask new professionals. A few people will indicate yes. But the percentage of those who recognize that at least part of their job involves sales is small. "I'm not in sales, so why do I need to learn how to sell and negotiate?" is a very common response.

I admit this is a bit of a trick question, but it is crucial to recognize that everyone is in sales. Your primary function may not be to sell products and services, but everyone needs to sell their ideas, their points of view, and their abilities. You are always selling (or negotiating) something, no matter your role or job function.

Learn to recognize the opportunities when you employ these skills. Such times may be the greatest opportunities for career advancement.

Customer awareness

You can gain customer awareness or adopt a customer-focused mindset, no matter what your role in an organization. You may think about customers and clients as being the people who buy the goods or services that your organization has to offer. That's the concrete definition of a customer or client. Remember "customers" or "clients" include any person or organization that you or your organiza-

TIP

You are always selling your ideas, your point of view, your opinion, your reputation, or your specific abilities. No matter your role in an organization, you are in sales, at least part-time.

tion serves. For you, your customers might be co-workers if you provide an internal support function for your organization such as technology or accounting.

What is customer awareness? It includes clearly identifying your customer(s) and learning everything you can about them. You also need to understand how your role relates to sales in your organization. How do you get more people to consume the products or services your organization produces? Do you encourage people to read a blog, vote for your candidate, support your policies, subscribe to your research, buy your advertising space, or return as patients to your practice? All of these efforts relate to the sales process and are central to customer awareness.

TIP

Should you consider your boss as a client? Every day you are selling the value that you bring to your organization. Remember what the best sales people know: ask questions, carefully listen, create solutions, professionally present solutions, and provide follow-up. Does this sound like a good way to interact with your boss or manager?

Even if you are not in a formal sales function, you may at times be asked to participate in client meetings, tradeshows, and presentations. Everyone from graphic designers to nurses to entry-level marketing staff members will occasionally participate in meetings with customers, clients, patients, etc. If you're attending a sales meeting, learn all you can about the customer beforehand.

LACK OF CUSTOMER AWARENESS

A high level of customer awareness is critical in all situations. Here are some scenarios to avoid:

• Driving a Hertz rental car to a meeting with an Avis customer. (You might also want to hide your Kia in the parking lot, if your meeting is with Ford.)

• Ordering a Pepsi for lunch with a client from Coca-Cola. (Although, it's likely that the Coca-Cola people wouldn't eat lunch in a restaurant that served Pepsi.)

• Sending a FedEx package to your customers at UPS.

• Wearing a Burberry scarf to a presentation at L.L. Bean.

While it may seem implausible, these scenarios happen often, especially to new professionals who haven't yet developed their customer awareness.

How does your role relate to sales in your organization?

Do you understand how your role relates to the sales function of your organization? Remember "sales" includes the delivery of goods or services. For example, if you work for a non-profit that runs sports camps for at-risk, inner-city youth, "sales" might include the programs at the camp. If you work for a national political campaign, "sales" may include a voter-registration drive or a town hall meeting.

Even if your job function doesn't directly involve sales, when you are a part of any business organization that sells products or delivers services, it is important to have a high-level understanding of the sales function or the way your organization delivers it's products or services. The sales function is the engine that drives every organization. Delivering products or services to customers, clients, and constituents is at the core of the mission for every company, government agency, school, or nonprofit organization. Sometimes even the smartest new professionals don't realize that everything they do in the workplace is related to sales or the delivery of a service. That service may include healthcare, government regulation, entertainment, or consulting. If you're in a marketing role, you're providing your sales team with the materials they need to sell or market a product. If you write for a print magazine, your stories help sell your magazine's brand to advertisers.

The table below shows how some common job roles relate to the sales function in an organization.

JOB ROLE	HOW ROLE RELATES TO SALES FUNCTION
Marketing assistant	Provides print, radio, and television advertising to support sales team.
Magazine writer	Produces content which increases subscribers, which in turn attracts advertisers.
Accountant	Keeps track of sales, costs, and expenses related to products, services, and personnel.
Administrative assistant	Assists in tasks related to sales of products and services offered by the company.
Engineer	Delivers expertise in the form of engineering services.
Business analyst	Analyzes sales and economic data to assist the sales force.
Doctor or nurse	Provides expertise to deliver healthcare services.

If you're a counselor at a nonprofit organization, you come face-to-face daily with various clients. A politician's constituents are important clients because without their votes, he or she doesn't get elected. If you work in a doctor's office, the way you care for the patients will reflect on the physician's professional brand. Patients will return to the practice if they like the way they are treated.

Remember that everything you do in your workplace is, in some way, affecting sales of your organization's products and services. Without sales, your organization probably would not exist. If you haven't already done so, figure out your role in your company's sales structure and how it impacts clients, customers, constituents, patients, students, and others. I guarantee that if your organization uses formal performance appraisals, it will measure your direct or indirect contribution to the organization's primary purpose—the delivery of goods or services to its customers, clients, or constituents.

Using sales and negotiation skills in your own career

There are many opportunities in your career to employ the same underlying skills used by the salesperson at the car dealer or the telemarketer who tries to convince you to switch television services. If you've convinced yourself that you are not in "sales," how will you recognize these opportunities as just that—opportunities?

Still not convinced? Take a look at the following lists and decide how many of these situations you're likely to encounter over your career.

Sales

- Selling your skills in a job interview.

- Pitching your ideas to a client.

- Selling your work product—making the case that your report/presentation/analysis/design is better than your colleague's.

- Demonstrating your organization's potential value to an angel investor.

Negotiations

- Justifying a salary increase.

- Seeking an internal job change.

- Convincing your manager that you deserve a promotion.

- Persuading your boss that you've earned some additional vacation.

- Requesting access to a training program or reimbursement for a part-time MBA.

- Making the case for you to work flexible hours.

If you are not in a formal sales function, you probably have no training in negotiations or sales skills. It's up to you to become familiar with the basics so that you can sell yourself, your work, and your ideas or to negotiate with managers, clients, and vendors.

Developing negotiation skills

There is a lot of overlap between the skills you use for sales and those you use to negotiate. Both are art forms that also include specific techniques that can be employed to track, manage, and complete the transaction (otherwise known as "close" the sale). But neither is a science with exact steps and a "one size fits all" solution. Good negotiation skills provide a great foundation for developing good sales skills.

With both sales and negotiations, remember that you will improve with practice. Like the other skills in this book, sales and negotiation skills can be learned and practiced.

Basic principles for good negotiations include:

- Fostering a win-win attitude for all parties involved.

- Asking GOOD questions and being a GREAT listener.

- Taking the time necessary to intelligently consider offers.

- Being flexible and looking for compromise solutions.

- Recognizing the negotiation styles and techniques being employed by others.

- Understanding the cultural issues at play. Organizational cultures and personal cultures (nationality or ethnicity-based) may play a role in negotiations.

You may have had the opportunity to practice your negotiation skills as you entered the job market. Think back to when you were first interviewing. You were the product that you were trying to sell. You did your best to sell your skills and accomplishments to a prospective employer. You presented your resume and explained your past achievements. You demonstrated how you would be a valuable member of the team.

Then the job offer came. Did you immediately accept the initial offer? Or, did you negotiate for such things as a higher salary, more vacation time, a delayed start-date, or an early end-date? If you successfully negotiated for and got any of these additional perks, congratulations! That's why it's just as important to know how to negotiate, as it is to know how to sell. In today's workforce, mastering this skill means that you are already farther ahead of most of your peers.

> **TIP**
>
> *Compromise is the key to successful negotiations and the foundation for a lasting professional relationship.*

There are many other times during your professional career that sales and negotiation skills will be valuable. For example, if your organization doesn't provide annual pay raises and you may need to negotiate your own salary increase. You need to sell your skills on a day-to-day basis in a subtle way within the office environment. You want your manager to easily recognize the value you bring to the organization. Demonstrating what you can do, and doing it well is part of selling yourself.

Even if you don't work in the sales department, you probably participate—directly or indirectly – in support of the sales team. Another scenario is when you are negotiating a service with an outside vendor. If you're in the marketing department, you may be hiring a videographer, a photographer, or a web developer. You might need to negotiate with such vendors, perhaps convincing them to accept the budgeted fee. A photographer, for example, might be willing to work for less money if he or she can shoot all the photographs that you need during one morning. Negotiating successfully with a vendor benefits your organization—as well as your career.

INTER-OFFICE NEGOTIATIONS

Even within the same company you may negotiate a partnership between your division and another. For example, you might agree to certain tasks in exchange for tasks that will be completed by the other division. The technology division could agree to create a website to promote the product that your division will be marketing if your division provides all of the content, including the graphics and videos.

Within the first few years of your career, you may be in a position where you're interviewing staff and negotiating salaries. You may be creating partnerships, both inside and outside your firm. If you work for a pharmaceutical company, for example, you might be expected to negotiate a multi-million-dollar contract with an advertising agency to promote a new medication. You could find yourself responsible for locating office space and negotiating the terms of a lease.

TIP

Sales rarely occur without some form of negotiations.

The more complex the sale, the more negotiations are involved. If you're in a sales role for your company, you may have already noted that the negotiations portion of a sales cycle happens once the customer or client is persuaded to buy your product or service. Typically, that involves other points related to the transaction that could include:

- Payment terms

- Delivery dates and deadlines

- Prices and discounts

- Concessions

- Guarantees or warranties

- Method of delivery

- Quality assurance

TIP

People like to do business with people they like—this is the most important part of any negotiations or sales process.

Here are some basic tips that are used by the best sales people and negotiators:

- Ask questions about your prospective client's challenges and problems.

- Listen carefully to what your customer says, so that you develop a true understanding of their situation and needs.

- Create and deliver solutions that solve your customer's challenges.

- Present your solutions in a professional manner, both verbally and in a written proposal.

- Provide regular follow-up with existing customers, establishing a professional relationship bond and demonstrating the value of being your business partner.

FORMAL SALES METHODS AND TECHNIQUES

Businesses often follow specific professional sales methodologies—such as the Sandler method, the Dale Carnegie philosophy, and others. If you are in a formal sales or business development role, learn which methodologies are popular or favored by your organization. If the firm hasn't adopted a methodology, consider using the one your boss uses or the one used by the most successful salesperson.

Here is a list of some well-known sales techniques and processes—there are thousands. If you want to expand your base of knowledge on sales and negotiation skills, investigate any of them. ✗

• Sandler Sales Training Seminars

• Dale Carnegie® Seminars

• *SPIN Selling*® by Neil Rackam

• *The New Solution Selling* by Keith Eades

• *New Strategic Selling* by Stephen Heiman and Diane Sanchez

• *Hope is Not a Strategy* by Rick Page

• *Advanced Selling Strategies* by Brian Tracy

In generations past, many good sales people did not consider their skills a legitimate career because they weren't skills learned in college. But, in today's world, a sales career is a highly valued profession. Many universities and colleges, including Harvard, now offer courses in sales. The annual National Collegiate Sales Competition, at Kennesaw State University in Georgia, draws students from Canada, the USA, and Mexico. ✗

Members of the sales force, or the client-focused division, of your organization are often paid very well—sometimes even more than the CEO. This is another reflection of the importance of this function and a reason that you may want to further investigate this career track.

ACCELERATE YOUR CAREER EXPERIENCE - NEXT STEPS

1. Are you convinced by now that everyone is in sales? If not, read *To Sell is Human,* by Daniel Pink.

2. Define for yourself and write down answers to the following:

- What product or service does your organization "sell"?

- How does your current role relate to delivering these products or services to your customer, clients, constituents, or patients?

- What specific skills do you use in support of the primary sales function? Which of these skills can you improve?

3. Identify three situations in the last twelve months in which you have applied sales or negotiation skills. Possibilities include selling an idea, convincing someone to adopt your viewpoint or approach, negotiating a raise or promotion, negotiating terms with a vendor, or selling your product or service to a customer.

4. Identify three possible situations where you will apply sales and negotiation skills in the next twelve months. How will you prepare for these situations?

5. Attend a Karrass Effective Negotiating® public seminar or an American Management Association (AMA) course. Upon successful completion, you will earn a recognized credential in a critical skill area.

ADDITIONAL RESOURCES ✘

To Sell is Human—The Surprising Truth About Moving Others by Daniel H. Pink

Why? Ranked a top seller by the New York Times, Washington Post and The Wall Street Journal, *To Sell is Human* explains sales in a way that applies to everyone—in every field. Pink, the author of *Drive* and *A Whole New Mind*, is an exceptional writer and lays out a convincing argument as to why "moving others" is a critically important skill in your career and your life.

Go-Givers Sell More
by Bob Burg and John David Mann

Why? Bob Burg and John David Mann, the national best selling authors of *The Go-Giver: A Little Story About A Powerful Business Idea*, explore five principles that everyone can apply in their professional lives as you interact with co-workers, clients, managers, constituents, etc. These are The Laws of Value, Compensation, Influence, Authenticity, and Receptivity.

Karrass Effective Negotiating Seminars

Why? For more than 40 years, Karrass has been a leader in providing negotiation training through their public two-day seminars offered throughout the world. Dr. Chester Karrass, the founder, has also written several books including *In Business as in Life— You Don't Get What You Deserve You Get What You Negotiate* and *Negotiating Effectively Within Your Organization*.

American Management Association (AMA)

Why? The AMA currently offers approximately two dozen seminars that cover the practical, hands on aspects of sales and negotiations delivered via classroom, live online, and on-demand. If you work for an organization that is a member of the AMA or the Federal Government, a discount may be available.

7

ORGANIZATIONAL AWARENESS

Every company has two organizational structures: the formal
one is written on the charts; the other is the everyday relationship
of the men and women in the organization.

HAROLD S. GREEN

In this chapter, you will learn:

• What is organizational awareness.

• Why organizational awareness is important to your career.

• How to increase your organizational awareness using a simple framework.

What is organizational awareness?

Organizational awareness is the understanding of your organization from top to bottom and from inside to out. It enables
you to understand how you and your role relate to the larger
organization and industry in which you work. It also includes
the way in which your organization relates to the global economy. Understanding your organization will help you navigate
your career.

Organizational awareness includes the culture, politics, and
the written and unwritten rules that shape your day-to-day
work and your long-term professional aspirations. Knowing
your organization includes knowing the players—your col-

leagues. You also should understand the external forces that impact your organization and everyone in it—competitors, industry trends, government policies, economics, and other global dynamics.

It is important to note that the term "organizational awareness" has a variety of meanings depending on the context. In this book, the focus is on your awareness and understanding of your role in relation to your team, organization, industry/sector, the larger economy/marketplace/country, and the world.

Maintaining your organizational awareness is an ongoing process. This is a challenging skill for everyone to develop, especially for recent graduates. As a student, you attended class, did your work, and were compensated with an appropriate grade in a pure meritocracy. Trends, culture, and politics in the surrounding environment had little to no impact on the evaluation of your work and resulting grades. For example, in your biology class you were immune from the impact of the science department's decision to implement a hiring freeze while the sociology department decided to expand its faculty. And you would certainly not consider changing your major because of organizational decisions like these. In the workplace, factors like these are more important to your career.

As a professional, the forces in your organization and the surrounding environment have a much greater impact on your work and your career path. A high-level of organizational awareness is crucial. As you progress in your career, this skill will become second nature, but don't get complacent. Even at advanced levels in your career, organizational awareness is vital.

YOUR ROLE IN THE ORGANIZATION

The definition of organizational awareness starts with you and your role as they relate to the broader environment that includes your team, your organization, the industry, and the broader market/economy.

In order to understand yourself and your role in this context, study the other forces that shape your professional environment. Organizations are made up of people and you won't fully understand your environment without understanding the people in it. The two are tightly linked. Finally, understand the written and unwritten rules of the organization including how success is measured, how performance is measured, and how performance appraisals are conducted.

Why is organizational awareness important to your career?

When working with or for any organization, understanding the context in which you work is vital. Your success or failure will depend on it. While all of the skills covered in this book are important, this one is absolutely necessary for your professional survival. There is a Darwinian aspect to this skill: If you don't adapt to your professional environment, you will likely become extinct.

Think about your college experience. How successful would you have been if you never figured out how each professor assessed your work and determined grades for their courses? Would you have graduated if you weren't aware of those varied requirements? How would your experience have been different if you didn't understand the relationship between the academic department in which you majored and the department where you earned your minor?

How do you acquire organizational awareness?

Achieving and maintaining organizational awareness requires an ongoing effort because the environment is constantly changing. Consider this work an ongoing research project that will last your entire career. You will need to continually evaluate yourself, your workplace environment, your co-workers, and your boss. This skill—your ability to monitor the elements of the workplace environment and adapt accordingly—will become second nature as you become an experienced professional.

When you transition to a new organization or a new industry, this skill will have a renewed importance as you adapt to your new professional environment.

I recommend a simple framework for organizing information about your professional environment—a set of five concentric circles. In this framework, you occupy the center ring, your business unit or team is the next ring, and your organization is the third ring. Picture a typical bulls eye target.

There are many ways to organize your framework and this makes the most sense to me. Feel free to come up with your own and use whatever framework or method of collecting, monitoring, and organizing information that makes sense to you.

THE BULLS-EYE FRAMEWORK

There are five concentric circles in this framework with you in the center ring. The five circles include:

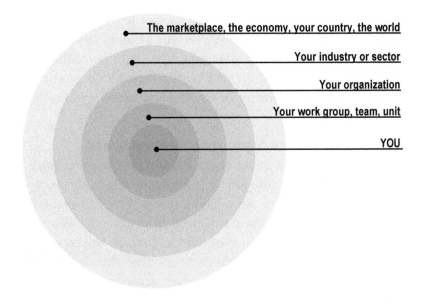

The marketplace, the economy, your country, the world

Your industry or sector

Your organization

Your work group, team, unit

YOU

Industry →	Government	Healthcare	For Profit	Non-profit
1. Work group	Supply specialists	ICU nurses	Capital markets	Social workers
2. Organization	U.S. Navy	Hospital	JPMorgan	American Red Cross
3. Industry	Military	Healthcare	Financial services	Nonprofit
4. Economy	World	U.S. and International	US and International	U.S. and International

Circle #1: YOU

Do you work for a large organization with multiple divisions, branches, or subsidiaries? Add another circle between circles #2 and #3 to account for that additional layer of complexity. Alternatively, if you are an entrepreneur working in a five-person start-up, then remove Circle #2 because there is a direct connection between you and the top level of your company. This framework is simple and flexible to accommodate your situation.

Circle #2: Your Work Group, Team, and Unit

Your work group, team, or business unit is the group of people with whom you spend most of your time. It may be a small team of five people or a large group of fifteen or more. You are generally doing the same type of work and you will spend a lot of time with these people. This group—which includes your boss, supervisor, or manager—is important because these individuals will have the greatest impact on your success. Your ability to effectively work with your boss and your colleagues will have a large influence on your career success.

Learn as much as you can about each colleague. Take a genuine interest in their success and most likely they will do the same for you. Understand the strengths and limitations of your co-workers, as well as their values and cultures. Using the self-awareness you gain from the assessments like the ones presented in Chapter 9: Executive Presence chapter, try to understand where your skills, preferences, and work style complement your team and where there may be a conflict. Increased self-awareness is helpful, but don't assume too much or project your self-awareness onto others.

It is usually obvious how your work contributes to your group, but do you understand your manager's goals, work styles, and priorities? This is where it starts to get complicated. It's reasonable to expect your manager's performance to be measured based on the work of the group he/she manages. But that's not always the case, especially in larger organizations. The result can be changing priorities and focus. Your supervisor could be part of a matrix-reporting structure where she is accountable to two different managers and measured by different criteria.

KNOW YOUR MANAGER

Why is it important to know your manager? Because you will interact with this person on a day-to-day basis and he or she is likely to be one of your best allies. For example, if your manager gets a promotion, he or she may help you move up in your organization, too. In the beginning, though, understand your manager's needs, priorities, and work style. Part of your job is to help your boss shine in the organization.

HOW DOES YOUR TEAM RELATE TO THE LARGER ORGANIZATION? In very large organizations, there might be multiple levels (business units, subsidiaries, regional divisions, country offices) between your immediate work group and the top level of the organization. Make sure to understand the hierarchy. Put your immediate group in where it fits within the context of the entire organization.

Is your business unit expanding or contracting compared with others? Is your team meeting its goals compared with other groups? Is your group duplicating the work of another group? What is your team's role in the sales process (see Chapter 6: Sales and Negotiation Skills)? How is your manager viewed within the organization—as a leader among leaders or as a newcomer?

These questions represent a small sample of the type of information you should be actively seeking and analyzing. ✗

IS TEAMWORK IMPORTANT?

Yes. Yes. Yes. There. Enough said. But wait, there's more. . .

Teamwork is generally considered one of many soft-skills in career development. Like many other skills introduced in this book, teamwork is challenging to teach or learn from a book. Volumes have been written on the subject. No book alone is enough to learn this skill without actual experience.

I've included this very brief discussion about teamwork while discussing Circle #2: Your Work Group, Team, or Unit. This is where you will use your teamwork skills. You will practice and hone these skills in your day-to-day work. Those who have participated in team sports, the military, or other team-based competitions have some familiarity, but teamwork in a professional setting has its own unique dynamics. The bottom line is this. . . . teamwork matters.

If you don't have experience working in a team setting, you may struggle when first immersed in this situation. Well-functioning teams usually produce better output but that is not always the case. Here are some very general guidelines:

- Be assertive without being domineering.

- Listen and understand before speaking.

- Expect to do some negotiating and compromising.

- The team comes before any individual (unless your boss is part of the team, then all bets are off).

Teamwork in a professional setting can be exciting. A team environment is often where stars are born and others fade away. The importance of every topic, question or issue, no matter how small or trivial, can be magnified when you add the personalities of the team into the mix.

The single best piece of advice about working in a team is from the old adage: There is no "I" in the word "team." It is a cliché, but it's true.

Here is a scenario to illustrate: Let's say that you are a social media strategist for an online retail company. Your role is to create and carry out a social media plan using Facebook, Twitter, and Pinterest. During your first year on the job, the vice president of marketing tells you that social media will now be integrated into the company's major marketing plan. At your first marketing team meeting, you are told that the messaging you developed doesn't match well with the overall plan. You are asked to rewrite it.

You could attempt to convince the entire marketing team that they don't understand social media and, therefore, the messaging that you developed should stand on its own. Alternatively, you could ask questions about the overall marketing plan, listen carefully to the answers, and revise your messaging to better fit.

This discussion of teamwork and the scenario above illustrate a much larger point. Teamwork matters in every organization. And being a good team player means you need to understand Circle #1 and Circle #2. The relationship between the two builds or breaks the team.

Circle #3: Your Company or Organization

You'll want to understand and be able to articulate how your role (Circle #1) and the work of your team, group, business unit (Circle #2) relates to your organization (Circle #3). It is challenging for anyone beginning in a new organization to "connect the dots" in this way. You can't really gain the depth of understanding by simple observation. It requires diligent study and thorough analysis.

Such study and analysis will pay off. Gaining a deep understanding of your role in the larger context of both your team and your organization (and all of the layers in between) helps put your work into context. You will understand how your effort contributes to the mission of the organization. You will probably experience more meaning in your work and be more satisfied with your job—always a good outcome. You will also be more attuned to the organization's priorities, which become your boss's priorities and ultimately yours. Being aware of these priorities will help keep you focused. Finally, by understanding how your work fits into the larger picture, you will be able to identify synergies, opportunities, challenges, or conflicts.

Let me illustrate that last point. Let's say your first job after college is working for a multi-national engineering firm. Your role is to maintain and update the content of the organization's website. Your boss oversees several technology teams including website, desktop support, and intranet. Your boss reports directly to the head of IT for the whole organization. She is responsible for the entire technology infrastructure including servers, accounting and human resources systems, and disaster recovery. Of course, the IT department also supports the technology needs of the entire organization, as well as its customers and business partners.

Your organization hires a new CEO whose role is twelve levels above yours in the organizational hierarchy. You research and learn that this new CEO started her career at Google. You find that in her last two CEO positions she converted both organizations to Google's cloud-based technology platform. After a few months as the CEO, she announces that your organization will adopt Google's platform. You're not surprised. You anticipated this change because you are plugged in to your organization.

Then you discovered that the current web technology is not compatible with Google's platform. You are able to highlight this to your manager who raises it to his manager. The IT department as a whole is recognized as adding value to the organization above and beyond their support function. And because of your foresight, you are seen as adding value above and beyond your role as the web content manager.

WHAT IS THE YOUR ORGANIZATION'S HISTORY?

Part of understanding your organization is to understand its history, culture, and values. Researching the history of your organization is usually straightforward. Private organizations may have been covered by the print or online media, so look to those sources for historical information. Check public records for historical information about public companies with financial reporting requirements, government agencies, or other public entities. Research the organization itself and its leadership. The history of an organization is created every day, so pay particular attention to major events in the history of your organization such as a merger, buyout, bankruptcy, a scandal, legal action, natural disaster, or other major event (i.e., September 11, 2001). What impact, positive and negative, did the event have on the values and culture of the organization?

> **TIP**
>
> *The history of an organization is informative, but it does not predict the future direction with 100 percent certainty. The history of an organization is created every day.*

Look for trends, themes, and discrepancies between the organization's history and its current operations. Is the organization maturing or is it stuck in the past? While the history of an organization is informative, it does not predict the future direction with 100 percent certainty.

WHAT ARE THE VALUES AND CULTURE OF THE ORGANIZATION?

Discovering the values and culture of an organization is more challenging than researching its history. Values and culture are difficult to pinpoint exactly. Time spent exploring this facet of organizational awareness is well worth it. The values and culture of an organization can impact your long-term satisfaction. You are likely to be more satisfied if your organization's values and culture are compatible with your own.

YOUR ORGANIZATION - A FAMILY ZONE?

Does your organization include members of the same family? This is often the case in private organizations that began as family businesses. Multiple family members in an organization have the potential to dramatically shape the organization's values and culture.

KNOW THE PLAYERS

Every organization is the sum total of its people. I cannot emphasize this enough. To know the people in your organization is to understand the organization. Know the players within your organization and your industry. These people will directly and indirectly influence your career. Study them. Connect with them. Learn from them.

FIND A MENTOR

As you get to know the people in your organization and industry, seek out a few mentors. You don't have to formalize a mentor-mentee relationship for it to be beneficial. Look for people who have forged a path congruent with your own career goals. If your organization offers a formal mentoring program, be sure to take advantage of this valuable resource. ✗

Learn about the leaders of your organization. Use social media wisely and don't venture into that creepy, stalker place. LinkedIn is considered the place for professional networking, so all information there is fair game. You will never be accused of snooping if you rely on public media sources. Look for print, television, or online interviews with the leaders of your organization. Many CEOs and other leaders write books or have books written about them. These are excellent sources of insight into the people who lead your organization.

Here is a simple test of your knowledge: Could you have a timely and relevant discussion with the CEO or other senior leaders of your organization right now? What questions would you ask? What would you say? Do you share anything in common that you could discuss—a hobby, a hometown, or an alma mater?

Where there are people, there are politics. Workplace politics are about the way people interact with one another and advance their individual agendas. Think of a person's agenda as the issues he or she professes to care about. What people care about drives their motivation. Some people are looking for a promotion while others are looking to save their jobs. Some are advocating for their customers while others are heeding the government regulators. Understand people's agendas to better understand them. Be aware that agendas vary by person and by situation. Agendas are not always what they seem on the surface.

GOOGLE THE CEO – KNOW HIM OR HER BY SIGHT

I learned one of the most important lessons of my career during an intensive, three-month training program at JP Morgan. The lesson didn't take place in a classroom but instead in the elevator.

It was Friday on a warm summer day and I was returning from lunch with two other trainees. We were in a great mood from lunch and were cracking some jokes and laughing in the elevator on our way to our next training session.

Just before the elevator doors closed, three people stepped inside. I instantly recognized one of them as Sir Dennis Weatherstone, the CEO and chairman of the bank, who was also knighted by Queen Elizabeth II. As he stepped into the elevator, I said hello and stepped to one side to make room.

My fellow trainees didn't recognize the CEO. They continued to joke and laugh. From where I was standing in the elevator, there was no way I could alert them. Weatherstone didn't say a word, but he casually glanced over his shoulder as he exited the elevator on the 19th floor—the executive level.

Later that afternoon, the director of our training program told the entire class that she had received a call from CEO's office about the unprofessional behavior from some of her training class. Let's just say, it didn't reflect well on her and she wasn't happy. And I never forgot the lesson from that day. Know your organization's leader by sight. ✗

UNDERSTAND THE RULES OF THE GAME

You'll encounter many important rules within your organization —formal and informal, written and unwritten. These "rules of the game" dictate how your performance is measured. How well you navigate them can hold you back or help you get ahead.

In college, you were given a grade at the end of the course that represented your performance for that class. The GPA on your resume is the measurement of your overall performance in all of your college classes. As a professional, your performance appraisal or performance review is your new report card or GPA.

Performance appraisals are vital in most organizations. Much of your professional development and success will depend on them. Some organizations will provide you with an evaluation after three months of employment; others will not do it for a year or more.

There are various types and formats for each organization and within each industry. Some common types of appraisals include: 360-Degree Feedback, Management by Objectives (MBO), third party appraisals, top-down assessments, self-assessment, forced ranking, or rating scale. These may also be used in combination with one another.

No matter the type of performance appraisal your organization uses, knowing the answers to these questions will help you be prepared:

- Are performance appraisals formal or informal?

- When will performance appraisals occur?

- As a new employee, when will you receive your first formal appraisal?

- How much do performance appraisals count toward compensation and promotions?

- Is there an opportunity for self-assessment?

Ideally, your performance appraisal should contain no surprises. Hopefully your manager is providing feedback along the way. Likewise, you should seek feedback throughout the year so you can continually improve. Don't wait until your performance appraisal to find out you're not meeting expectations.

PREPARING FOR YOUR PERFORMANCE APPRAISAL

To help yourself when it comes time for your performance appraisal, maintain a record of your accomplishments throughout the year. You are often required to provide input to your performance appraisal in the form of a self-assessment or a response to your manager's assessment. Be prepared. On at least a monthly basis, reflect for 15 to 30 minutes about your recent accomplishments and write them down.

As you record the details of you accomplishments over the previous month, be specific. Quantify as much as possible. This document is for your own purposes only, so it does not need to be formal. Just keep a record for yourself. Here are some ideas and examples to prompt you:

- Record that you completed three projects resulting in $75,000 in revenue and that your sales revenue exceeded quota by 15 percent. Or, you might report that you launched two products and wrote three grant proposals for a total of $1,000,000 in funding.

- Make a note of the colleagues you assisted and projects involved.

- Make a note of the job candidates you recruited or interviewed. For example, say that you interviewed five candidates, three of whom joined the organization.

- Record any professional development that you've undertaken on your own. Did you earn a certificate in a MOOC that is relevant to your field? Did you earn your Competent Communicator designation from Toastmasters?

MY FIRST SELF-ASSESSMENT

The first time I was asked to write a formal self-assessment was a full year after I had started at my first post-college job. It had been a busy year that included graduating from college, moving to New York City, finding a roommate and an apartment, and completing a three-month training program.

The first question on the self-assessment was: "Describe your accomplishments over the last year." I was stumped. I had accomplished a lot, but I didn't know how to begin answering that question.

In addition to keeping an ongoing record of your professional accomplishments, I recommend that you save hard copies of your performance appraisals at home. Your past performance appraisals will be useful when you write your appraisal next year. In addition, they are a good source of materials for updating your LinkedIn profile. It's a good idea to keep copies at home because you may not remember or may not be able to retrieve them if you leave your organization. Remember, your performance appraisal is your new report card.

TIP

One of the keys to advancing in an organization is to ask for additional responsibility. Do this in a private meeting or in a note to your manager. Tell your boss that you are willing to do more work. But first, make sure you are doing your own job well.

Circle #4: Your Industry or Sector

At this level, focus your attention on how your organization fits within the industry in which it operates. Understand the relative size in terms of people, dollars, and the influence of your organization compared with others in the industry. Who are your competitors? Which organizations are considered the industry leaders or emerging leaders? Who are considered superstars or experts? Also, you should examine related industries. If you work in the auto industry, for example, you should also follow the oil and gas industry.

Sources of information include trade journals, public and private research reports, blogs, books/podcasts about the industry and its leaders, and industry-based LinkedIn Groups. Trade associations are an especially valuable source of information. Many offer free or discounted membership for young professionals.

Circle #5: The Economy and/or Global Marketplace

The local, national, and world economy impacts every organization and every professional from the solo entrepreneur to the CEO of the largest multinational. It is imperative to stay current with the news, events, and macro-trends that could impact Circles #1-4. For many organizations, the greatest impact from Circle #5 relates to developments in global economics and politics.

LARGE NUMBER FLUENCY

How many zeroes are in a trillion? How many billions are in one trillion? What percentage of one billion is one million?

To understand much of the information in Circle #5: The Economy and/or Global Marketplace, you have to be fluent in large numbers. Outside of the professions related to science, most of the big numbers you will encounter will involve economics, money, or populations. To be fluent, you must know the relative size of large numbers and be able to analyze their significance. ✘

Sources for this information are mostly obvious. They include newspapers, news magazines, blogs, economic reports, current business books, and podcasts.

ACCELERATE YOUR CAREER EXPERIENCE - NEXT STEPS

1. Read and understand your organization's public financial reports. You should be able to identify how your role in the organization adds to the financial bottom line. Have a colleague who majored in accounting walk you through the top-line numbers and identify any trends, major changes, etc.

2. Know the names of the senior management in your organization and be able to recognize them by sight. You never know whom you'll meet in the elevator. Be able to hold a relevant and timely discussion about the organization at any time. Before you meet them, learn about them on LinkedIn, Google, and from other public sources.

3. Network within your own organization. Starting with fellow alumni. Networking provides an opportunity to learn about other parts of the organization and builds your professional network at the same time. Set a goal for yourself—meet someone new once a week. Learn about their role and how they contribute to the organization's mission.

4. Look for opportunities to volunteer for cross-functional committees, on-campus recruiting, or volunteer projects sponsored by your employer. This is a great way to meet people in your organization that you otherwise might not. Volunteering also makes you a valuable team player.

5. Find and read any books written about your organization, its leaders, your organizations competitors, partners, customers, or your industry. A visit to your library, local bookstore, or a quick Amazon.com search makes such books easy to find. You'll learn more inside the pages of such books than you would by working in the organization for years.

6. Identify any industry trade associations in which your organization participates. Use these groups for the networking opportunities and industry news.

7. If your job takes you to trade shows or conferences, take advantage of this opportunity to network within your industry, learn about competitors, and spot trends.

ADDITIONAL RESOURCES ✗

Hoovers

Why? Hoovers and its parent company, Dun and Bradstreet (D&B), curate information for more than 85 million companies in 900 industries. Most information requires a paid subscription, but their website includes a lot of general business and company news and information.

Google Alerts

Why? This is a simple way to stay up to the moment about your organization, top management, your boss (if he or she is a newsmaker), business partners, competitors, and your industry. Create as many alerts as you need and always be "in the know." Use a system to archive (something other than your email inbox) the important information you want to save or review in the future.

American Society of Association Executives (ASAE)

Why? The ASAE's Gateway to Association directory provides a handy online search to identify relevant trade groups in your own industry.

8

YOUR PERSONAL BRAND

You never get a second chance to make a first impression

UNKNOWN

In this chapter, you will learn:

- Why your personal brand matters to your career.
- Why business etiquette is essential to maintain your personal brand.
- Why your "uniform" supports your personal brand.

Your Personal Brand

Generally speaking the term "personal branding" is the practice of positioning yourself as a commercial brand. Like Nike, Coke, Apple, you (as a professional) are also a brand. The definition of personal brand varies by industry and profession.

In a 1997 Fast Company article, "The Brand Called You," Tom Peters coined the phrase "personal branding" and declared, "Starting today you are a brand. You're every bit as much a brand as Nike, Coke, Pepsi, or the Body Shop." Peters, a business management expert, is also the co-author of the best selling book, *In Search of Excellence*, which many consider to be one of the most important business books ever written. ✖

To begin thinking of your professional self as a brand, ask yourself the following questions: What differentiates me as a professional? What qualities and capabilities do I want my colleagues and clients to associate with me as a professional?

Your personal brand in the workplace is how you define yourself as a professional and how you convey that definition to others. It is the standard you set and maintain for yourself. Equally important, your personal brand is how colleagues and clients see you as a professional. It is important to remember that there may be a gap between how you define your personal brand and how others perceive it.

You might also think of your personal brand as your professional reputation that includes the positive (and occasionally negative) qualities that people attach to you. For example, the late Steve Jobs, Mark Zuckerberg, Oprah, and Donald Trump all have well-know personal brands. What do you think of when you think of each person? The qualities that you associate with each make up their personal brands.

What do your colleagues think of when your name is mentioned? What three words do your customers associate with you as a professional? What is your professional reputation? Knowing the answers to these questions can make a significant difference in your own career.

Successful professionals are always working to manage and improve their personal brands. You should, too. But remember that you can't control what other people think of you, so focus on what you can control. While a high-quality personal brand alone will not guarantee success, a positive reputation will increase your chances. The most important thing to remember is that your personal brand can take years to build, but only moments to destroy. Building and protecting your personal brand should be a priority.

This chapter focuses on two specific aspects of personal brand—

> **TIP**
>
> *The most important thing to remember is that your personal brand can take years to build, but only moments to destroy.*

business etiquette and your image. Business etiquette is the way you act in a professional or workplace setting. There you are constantly judged by the way you interact with others. Your image is the way you look to others – the way you dress, groom, and present yourself.

As a new professional, these two aspects of your personal brand are an important part of your career foundation. You will enhance your career as you build and maintain your personal brand over the course of your professional life.

DEFINITION OF PERSONAL BRANDING.

Personal branding is the practice of people marketing themselves and their careers as brands...Personal branding also involves creating an asset by defining an individual's body, clothing, physical appearance, and areas of knowledge leading to a uniquely distinguishable, and ideally memorable, impression (Wikipedia).

Behavior in the workplace—business etiquette

Making the transition from college student to working professional is full of challenges. The rules and expectations are different. Some of the things you did on campus, in the classroom, and in the dining halls may not be acceptable in the workplace. Learning the practices of business etiquette can help ease you through the transition.

Knowing and following proper business etiquette is an essential part of building a solid personal brand. In most situations following the rules of etiquette is straightforward. You already know a lot about good manners. For example, you know not to talk with food in your mouth, wipe your nose with your shirtsleeve, or interrupt someone else's conversation.

Many resources cover basic good manners and business etiquette. You will find a number of references at the end of this chapter. If you don't already know and use these basics, learn them. Know them cold. That is a "no brainer." Arm yourself with this information, practice what you learn, and reap the benefits for the rest of your career.

Beyond the basics, proper business etiquette has many nuances. For example, you may not know how to address a high-ranking political figure from another country or which silverware to use for what course during a formal dinner. Self-awareness will help you here. The better you know yourself, the better you will do at navigating less-than-straightforward situations.

When you find yourself in unfamiliar territory observe those around you, especially more senior or experienced colleagues. If you are unsure about the protocol ask someone discreetly. When you are able to quietly admit what you don't know you are demonstrating a high level of self-awareness. Asking politely is far better than not asking and risking an etiquette blunder.

Today's professionals operate in a global economy. Sooner or later you will probably find yourself working with a client, colleague, or business associate from another country. You may find career opportunities overseas. Practicing interna-

TIP

Failure to demonstrate good business etiquette may indicate a lack of self-awareness. This could lead others to think that you also lack self-awareness in your business judgment.

tional business means that cultural, social, religious, and political overlays become more complex when it comes to proper business etiquette.

Three particularly important areas that call for proper business etiquette are introduction etiquette, technology etiquette, and dining etiquette.

THE ONE-ON-ONE INTRODUCTION

You never get a second chance to make a first impression. What kind of first impression will you make? Each time you introduce yourself to someone, a lot is riding on the first 30 seconds. And a lot can go wrong.

A common misstep is the dead fish handshake. It's an immediate turnoff when someone offers to shake your hand and it just lies there, lifeless. A handshake should be firm, but not too firm. You demonstrate good business etiquette when you don't try to show off your strength. Practice your handshake until it is just right.

A dead fish handshake is often accompanied by a lack of eye contact. In combination, a weak handshake and downcast eyes signal nervousness and a lack of self-confidence. It is normal to be nervous, especially in important situations, but a firm handshake and a direct look can help you hide those shaky nerves and establish a positive first impression.

The impression you create when meeting someone for the first time is when you begin to form your personal brand in that person's mind.

GUIDELINES WHEN MEETING SOMEONE

- Make your handshake firm and not too long or too short in duration.

- Look directly into the person's eyes and smile. There is no better way to say, "I am happy to meet you."

- Say your first and last name slowly and clearly when introducing yourself.

- Repeat the name of the person you are being introduced to saying: "It is nice to meet you, Bob (or Mary)." This has two benefits. First, it increases your chances of remembering their name. Second, people like the sound of their own name. ✗

TECH-ETIQUETTE

Etiquette related to technology is a whole new category of manners. When a six-ounce smart phone lets you speak to anyone from practically anywhere, stores 12,000 of your favorites songs, allows you to shoot photos and record videos, and enables you to access the Internet from anywhere, good manners are easy to forget.

For all these wondrous advantages, smart phones have created a major problem – they have turned many otherwise polite people into ungracious beasts. ✖ Don't fall into the trap and ignore common sense when it comes to your smart phone. Here is a list of dos and don'ts based on the most offensive and common mistakes:

- Turn off the ringer during meetings, events, and meals.

- Don't text or email during a meeting, unless absolutely necessary. If you must take a call or respond to a text, then excuse yourself and go to where you won't disturb the others. Keep the conversation or text chat brief.

- Don't discuss personal or confidential business information while on a cell phone in a public place.

- Do not keep glancing at your phone when you are with someone else. It may send the unintended message: "You are not important to me." This is not a good way to build professional relationships and it is not good manners.

TIP

Does your social media presence support your personal brand? Do you have photos and videos on Facebook or other social media sights that you wouldn't share with your manager or customers? If so, it's time to take them down or at least add some privacy settings.

ETIQUETTE AT MEALTIME

You may think your manners are good, but you can always learn something new. Your etiquette skills can be enhanced by awareness and practice. Proper etiquette is important in today's business world and not difficult to learn if you take the time.

TIP

If you are not sure which plate or utensil to use look for guidance from others at the table. If you need to, graciously ask for assistance in a lighthearted manner. You might say something to the person sitting beside you such as, "I'm never quite sure which is my bread plate and which is yours." Your companion will either politely clarify the situation, or admit to similar confusion. Either way, you've defused an awkward moment, demonstrated self-awareness, and learned something in the process.

Knowing the rules of mealtime etiquette allows you to focus on the deal, the sale, or the interview. Good manners can help you build rapport with the person across the table and focus on what the person is saying. You can't focus on the conversation or the other person if you're worried about which fork to use for your salad.

WHAT WOULD YOU DO?

Good manners and proper etiquette don't vary much. Once you have mastered the rules, you are armed with knowledge that will last your lifetime. Test yourself on the following situations, and check the answers at the end of the list:

1. **If given a choice, which fork should be used for your salad?**
2. **Should a cloth napkin be put in your lap the minute you sit down or once all of the guests have arrived?**
3. **Is your water glass to the left or the right of your plate?**
4. **If served ice cream for dessert during a formal dinner, where will you find your dessert spoon?**
5. **Once you've finished eating, where should your knife and fork be placed?**

See Link Library for the answers.

Your appearance—your image

Do you know your organization's professional "uniform?" Every organization and industry has a uniform. You should determine what that is. A formal dress code is not the same as your organization's uniform. Dress codes issued by the human resources department usually list the items you are not allowed to wear. Consider these the minimum standard—a starting point.

A survey taken by the National Association of Colleges and Employers (NACE) in 2005 found that 49 percent of employers would be strongly influenced in their opinion of a candidate wearing non-traditional attire.

An organization's leaders determine the organization's uniform. That doesn't necessarily mean your boss and it certainly does not mean your co-workers. You should dress like the people in the roles and jobs to which you aspire.

A good guideline is to dress like your boss's boss—the position at least two levels above you. That way, you are covered even if your boss isn't getting it right. It takes more than the right uniform to advance as a professional, but getting it wrong will harm your personal brand.

Be especially careful about popular fashion trends. Don't follow them blindly unless you work in one of the few industries where that is the norm. Be aware that the fashion industry is in the business of selling clothes. Don't count on fashion experts to dress you appropriately for work. When skinny ties or shorter skirts become the rage watch what the higher ups in your office are wearing before you invest in a new wardrobe. In the workplace, you should be known for the quality of the work you produce. In the business world, your clothes should be appropriate, not memorable.

DRESS RULES FOR THE WORKPLACE

- If you wear it to the beach, don't wear it to work.

- If you wear it to the bar on Saturday night, don't wear it in the office.

- Cheap suits are easy to spot. Make an investment in a well-fitted suit. A modestly priced suit can be tailored to fit well making it appear to be much higher quality.

- If it's in Vogue or Details, it's probably not appropriate for the office.

- Be current in style and age appropriate in your choices. Your business dress should be noticed for the right reasons and quickly forgotten.

- Avoid sloppiness, rips, and stains in any type of clothing and shoes.

- Don't wear a more expensive watch or carry a more expensive handbag than your boss. It sends the wrong message.

ACCELERATE YOUR CAREER EXPERIENCE – NEXT STEPS

1. Learn and practice business etiquette and good manners. This is one aspect of your professional brand that is easy to master. The rules of good manners are easily available and there is no excuse for getting this wrong. If you aren't completely certain that your level of business etiquette is at a 90% or higher level, then study up.

2. Look for other professionals with well developed workplace etiquette and watch how they conduct themselves.

3. Use the resources in the Additional Resources section to per-

fect your business etiquette. There is no such thing as being "too well-mannered."

4. Examine your professional wardrobe and be sure it supports the personal brand you want to develop. Make note how others in your organization and respected members of your industry dress. Observe how your boss's boss dresses. Pay particular attention during causal Fridays or other occasions when the dress code is business casual. Make it a game to figure out your organization's uniform.

ADDITIONAL RESOURCES ✖

Managing Brand You: Seven Steps to Creating Your Most Successful Self
By Jerry S. Wilson and Ira Blumenthal

Why? The seven steps in this book provide a roadmap for creating "Brand YOU" by employing the same concepts used in traditional commercial brand management such as brand attributes, brand essence, brand image, and brand insistence. Step one includes a brand audit to assess your current state and the book concludes with step seven, a detailed action plan to implement your Brand YOU. The authors have worked with some of the best brands on the planet including: Coca-Cola, McDonald's, Wal-Mart, Delta Airlines, and Marriott.

Branding Yourself
By Sherry Beck Paprocki and Ray Paprocki

Why? This guide is loaded with practical information about an array of issues related to building and enhancing your personal brand. It includes many examples of personal and commercial brands to emphasize the similarities of these concepts.

Kiss, Bow or Shake Hands (2nd Edition)
by Terri Morrison and Wayne A. Conaway

Why? In today's interconnected, international business world, you must understand the customs, business practices, and etiquette of your customers, clients, associates, and constituents. The world-wide edition includes details on more than 60 countries. There are also specific editions for Asia, Europe, Latin America. For each country, the book includes tips on doing business, a brief history of the country, and common business practices. It also gives pointers on negotiating, business entertaining, and protocol for greeting, gestures, and dress.

The Emily Post Institute

Why? Emily Post is synonymous with good manners. Her descendants have continued to publish etiquette books more than 50 years after her death. The Emily Post Institute offers many free resources including articles, blogs, monthly newsletters, and a YouTube channel with a great playlist called Etiquette Bites™. In addition to these free resources, there are low cost e-learning options for individuals and a bookstore. I recommend *The Etiquette Advantage in Business, Third Edition: Personal Skills for Professional Success* and *Manners in the Digital World: Living Well Online*.

The Essentials of Business Etiquette: How to Greet, Eat, and Tweet Your Way to Success
By Barbara Pachter

Why? This book includes 101 practical scenarios. It covers establishing rapport, maintaining a professional image, mealtime etiquette, and social media. These tips are based on real situations that professionals will encounter during their first year. As a professional, you cannot afford to make mistakes that could be easily avoided. This book will help you navigate the world of business etiquette.

Style Bible: What To Wear To Work
by Lauren A. Rothman

Why? Managing your professional wardrobe or "uniform" is challenging. There are many factors to consider including your own personal style and comfort, your organization's official and un-official dress codes, and current fashion trends. Rothman's *Style Bible* is an important resource for men and women who need to build and maintain a professional wardrobe. "Make sure you are dressing for the job you want, not just the one you have," is Roth-man's wisest advice.

9

YOUR EXECUTIVE PRESENCE

Knowing others is intelligence; knowing yourself is true wisdom.
Mastering others is strength; mastering yourself is true power.
If you realize that you have enough, you are truly rich.

LAO TZU, TAO TE CHING

In this chapter, you will learn:

- What executive presence is and what it means.

- Why executive presence matters even if you are not an executive.

- How personal branding relates to executive presence.

- The key components of executive presence and how to develop them.

I am not an executive, so why do I care?

"I am not an executive, nor do I want to be an executive, so why do I care about executive presence?" This is a common response from new professionals when discussing executive presence. Or maybe you would say, "I am an entrepreneur. My start-up doesn't have executives so executive presence doesn't matter."

I hear many variations of this same basic theme and my response is always the same executive presence matters! It matters in every industry, organization, job function, and role. From entry-level to the C-suite, this set of skills accounts for why some people are promoted over others, and why some entrepreneurs are able to raise capital while others struggle to get by.

Not yet convinced? Perhaps you are struggling with the word "executive" in the term, executive presence. If you prefer, use the term "professional presence." Everything else in this chapter will apply. Executive (or professional) presence will play a significant role in your career success.

Executive presence accounts for 26 percent of what it takes to get the next promotion, according to a 2012 study of 4,000 college graduate professionals in large corporations conducted by the Center for Talent and Innovation. ⚒ That means that at least one-quarter of "what it takes" to be successful in your career is based on something other than your job performance.

The study was done in large corporations, but what if you don't work for a large corporation? Is executive presence still important to your career? You bet it is! As a professional, your level of executive presence will matter to your investors, donors, board members, business partners, patients, managers, customers, and clients.

Executive presence can be a challenging concept for those who have spent four years in a college setting where they were rewarded with grades for their ability in a particular subject and the academic work they produced.

Think of your career in terms of a college course where 75% of your grade is based on the quality of your work and 25% is based on executive presence. Even if you were awarded full credit for the quality of your work, without executive presence, you'd earn only a grade of C.

Executive Presence vs. Personal Branding

You can establish a personal brand without having executive presence, but you can't have executive presence without an impeccable personal brand. Otherwise there are a number of similarities between these two essential concepts.

Think of any Hollywood celebrity regularly featured in the tabloids. These people have big personal brands, but they don't have executive presence. Now think of any successful entrepreneur, CEO, or other thought leader. Those individuals will have a personal brand and an executive presence. There is no denying that personal branding and executive presence are related, but executive presence is the higher-order skill. It requires a deep level of self-awareness.

What is executive presence?

Executive presence is a broad concept without a single definition. It can't be defined in a single, succinct sentence. Even though the definition is elusive, a new professional needs to become familiar with the concept of executive presence and its importance. It includes all of the other skills presented in this book and additional "soft skills" such as:

- Effective problem solving

- Effective decision making

- Critical thinking

- Planning, organizing, and prioritizing

- Team building and motivation

- Conflict management

- Stress management

- Risk management

Executive presence also includes qualities or characteristic that you don't learn from a book or in a classroom, but instead acquire through the experience of life. These include:

- Charisma

- Confidence

145

- Integrity

- Resilience

- Grit

- Adaptability

If you ask ten people to define executive presence, you will get ten different answers, but most answers will include many of these skills and characteristics. Whether your aspirations are to be an entrepreneur or to work in the C-suite of a Fortune 100 company, you must understand executive presence and how it impacts your career. It's that important!

To illustrate the challenge of determining a specific definition for executive presence consider how the following three experts describe the term.

Scott Eblin, author of *The Next Level*, defines executive presence this way: "First, it's about your ability to get results, especially when the expectations are continually changing. Second, it's about the behaviors you exhibit at the personal, team and organizational levels. When your behaviors align with the expected results, you have executive presence." �֍

In her book, *Speak Like A CEO*, Suzanne Bates describes executive presence as the "wow" factor that includes three dimensions: character, substance, and style. "What is intuitively understood about executive presence is that it's all about the capacity to mobilize others to act," Bates says. "At the core, it's necessary for influencing others. To become influential and lead large-scale, complex business initiatives, executive presence isn't a nice-to-have, but a must-have quality." ✖

John Beeson in a Harvard Business Review blog writes "Although executive presence is highly intuitive and difficult to pin down, it ultimately boils down to your ability to project mature self-confidence, a sense that you can take control of difficult, unpredictable situations; make tough decisions in a timely way and hold your own with other talented and strong-willed members of the executive team." ⚒

The way these three experts attempt to define executive presence indicates why this term can be elusive. In general terms, executive presence is the way you show up for work or your professional demeanor. It includes how you behave, how you interact with others, and how others perceive you. To complicate the concept further, executive presence will vary based on your level of seniority, your industry, and even your organization.

Executive presence cannot be reduced to a single skill. It is a collection of skills, qualities, and characteristics. However you define it, executive presence is vital to career success. Displaying executive presence every day will have a cumulative impact on your success. This is true for every industry, every role, and every level of experience.

How do you begin to build an executive presence?

Executive presence is a complex set of skills and characteristics that you will deepen and enhance throughout your career. Where do you start? How do you begin to build your executive presence? You begin with a solid foundation.

The foundation begins with gaining a deep understanding of your strengths, weaknesses, preferences, and work styles. As you reflect on these aspects of yourself in light of your professional goals, you will begin to craft your authentic executive presence, one that reflects your individuality.

So how do you acquire such deep knowledge of yourself as a professional? You begin by understanding and increasing your level of Emotional Intelligence (EI).

Emotional Intelligence (EI)

Emotional Intelligence (EI) is "the ability to identify, assess and control the emotions of oneself, of others, and of groups." (*A Dictionary of Psychology*, Coleman). Note that the term emotional intelligence (EI) is often used interchangeably with Emotional

Quotient (EQ). (For consistency, the term emotional intelligence or EI is used in this book.)

While emotional intelligence is not limited in scope, this chapter will focus on EI as it relates to your career or profession. For our purposes, the definition of emotional intelligence can be adapted as the ability to identify, assess, and control the emotions of yourself, your colleagues, clients, customers, constituents, and teams.

EI explains why people with average intelligence are easily able to outperform those with superior intelligence quotient (IQ) scores. EI can surprise and even frustrate recent graduates and new professionals used to an academic environment where EI has very little impact on a grade point average. The research in this area is conclusive—EI is a better predictor of professional success than IQ. In other words, your high GPA may have helped you get your first job, but it is not enough to make you successful.

The concept of emotional intelligence became widely popular in 1995 with the publication of Daniel Goleman's book, *Emotional Intelligence: Why it can matter more than IQ.* ✖ In a 1998 Harvard Business Review article, "What Makes a Leader?", Goleman applied the concept of EI to business. ✖ These are the five components of emotional intelligence:

- Self-awareness – the ability to recognize your moods, emotions, and drives, and their effect on others.

- Self-regulation – the ability to control or redirect disruptive impulses and moods; the propensity to suspend judgment and to think before acting.

- Motivation – a passion to work for reasons that go beyond money or status; a propensity to pursue goals with energy and persistence.

- Empathy – the ability to understand the emotional makeup of other people; skill in treating people according to their emotional reactions.

- Social skill – proficiency in managing relationships and building networks; an ability to find common ground and build rapport.

   How would you rate your abilities in each of these five components of EI? How much do you know about yourself and the way you interact with others in the workplace? How well do you see the relationship between EI and long-term career success? Once you acknowledge the importance of EI, you can begin making yours stronger.

How to get to know your professional self

To better understand yourself as a professional, there are a number of tools and assessments that you can use, some of which may be available for free or at a low cost through your college career center. Other assessments are available online. Three of the most popular and comprehensive assessments include:

- Meyers-Briggs Type Indicator®

- Clifton StrengthsFinder 2.0

- DiSC Behavioral Style Assessment

MYERS-BRIGGS TYPE INDICATOR®

The Myers Briggs Type Indicator is an assessment tool designed to reveal your personality type. This tool can indicate if you will be good at organizing tasks, creating and managing teams, training for leadership positions, resolving conflicts, motivating others, recognizing and rewarding others, and managing change within your organization. The results will be a type described with a combination of four letters according to your answers: introvert (I) / extrovert (E); sensing (S) / intuition (N); thinking (T) / feeling (F); and perceiving (P) / judging (J).

   When you understand your personality type, you can approach your own work in a manner that best suits your style. This may include how you manage your time, how you solve problems,

149

your best approaches to decision-making, and how you manage stress. Understanding your personality type can help you deal with workplace culture, the development of new skills, enhancing your interactions on teams, and coping with change in the workplace. If your work involves sales, understanding your personality type will also help you manage clients.

CLIFTON STRENGTHSFINDER 2.0

This online assessment tool, developed by Donald O. Clifton, an expert in strengths psychology, will help you determine your personality's strengths. Knowledge of these strengths can help you discover and develop your talents. This tool assesses thirty-four areas of strength, ranging from action orientation to analytical ability. Identifying your strengths will help you to mesh your skills with your career goals and lead you along the best professional path.

DiSC ASSESSMENT

DiSC is an acronym for Dominance (or Drive), Inducement (or Influence), Submission (Steadiness), and Compliance (Caution or Conscientiousness). The DiSC model is widely used in organizations around the world. It measures aspects of your personality and behavioral style in a variety of common workplace situations such as how you influence others, how you communicate with others, and how you respond to conflict.

No assessment is perfect and each has limitations, but these assessments can reveal important insights about you. The information gained could confirm something you might already suspect or highlight something about your personality of which you were not aware. These assessments will help as you develop your EI and in turn will serve as a foundation for your own executive presence.

ACCELERATE YOUR CAREER EXPERIENCE - NEXT STEPS

1. Based upon what you know now, take a few minutes to assess your current level of emotional intelligence in very general terms. How does executive presence play a role in your current position? How will it play a role in your long-term professional goals?

2. Think of three examples of when you demonstrated executive presence even if you didn't know the term before now.

3. Read at least one book on EI. Start with *Emotional Intelligence* by Daniel Goleman.

4. Explore the assessments recommended in this chapter. Consider the insights you gained by the output. What did you learn about yourself? What insight might you have gained about your colleagues, clients, or your manager? How will this new insight change the way you work or the way you approach your career?

ADDITIONAL RESOURCES ✗

Meyers-Briggs Type Indicator ®

Please Understand Me II: Temperament, Character, Intelligence by David Keirsey

Why? Keirsey provides quick access to the Meyers-Briggs Type Indicator with a 70-question assessment. The assessment will take you less time than it takes to drink a latte. The book includes profiles for each of the 16 type combinations. This simple exercise provides fascinating insights into your own personality and the personalities of your colleagues, customers, managers, and other people you interact with as part of your career.

*Type Talk at Work (Revised): How the 16 Personality Types
Determine Your Success on the Job*
by Otto Kroeger, Janet M. Thuesen, Hile Rutledge

Why? *Type Talk at Work* applies the principals of MBTI® to the
workplace. Using a method known as Typewatching, you will
learn how to apply the underlying psychology of the MBTI® to
yourself along with your colleagues, co-workers, managers, and
customers. The insight and skill gained will improve your communication ability and the quality of your professional relationships.

CPP, Inc.

Why? This company provides an online version of the MBTI® that
is more comprehensive than those provided in the books listed
above. There is a fee for the CPP's assessment.

Clifton StrengthsFinder

StrengthsFinder 2.0
by Tom Rath

Why? Based upon more than two million interviews, the Gallup
Organization has identified thirty-four themes of human talent.
Adaptability, connectedness, ideation, responsibility, and significance are a few examples. *StrengthsFinder* is a big proponent
of improving your existing strengths instead of improving your
weaknesses.

You also get an access code with the book that will allow you
to take the online assessment. This book is the updated version
based on the original *Now Discover Your Strengths* written by
Marcus Buckingham and Donald O. Clifton.

Emotional Intelligence (EI) / Emotional Quotient (EQ)

Emotional Intelligence
By Daniel Goleman

Why? This is the book that started it all. Goleman's bestseller goes well beyond the realm of work and your career, and it is well worth the read. Another great book by Goleman is *Working with Emotional Intelligence.*

TalentSmart

Why? TalentSmart provides online appraisals, coaching and consulting related to emotional intelligence. Drs. Travis Bradberry and Jean Greaves, co-authors of *Emotional Intelligence 2.0,* are leaders in this field. The TalentSmart website also includes very informative articles which will further your understanding of this fascinating field.

DiSC Behavioral Style Assessment

Why? There are several online resources available for the DiSC Assessment. Some are free versions with an abbreviated questionnaire with as few as a dozen questions.

10

CAREER-OLOGY IN PRACTICE

You have to be constantly reinventing
yourself and investing in the future.

REID HOFFMAN, LINKEDIN FOUNDER

The quote from Reid Hoffman, the founder of LinkedIn, serves as the perfect way to conclude this book. One of the underlying principles in this book is the idea of constantly reinventing yourself and investing in your future—the future of your career. Your professional development is just that. It is yours and it is up to you to determine how you advance it.

The concept of accelerating your own career experience offers a way to invest in your own professional development. You will recall there are four components of career experience including tenure, career skills, personal brand, and executive presence. You can apply the concept of accelerating your career experience to all of the components except tenure.

Take advantage of the discrepancy in the way the various components of experience are measured. Be intentional about identifying, acquiring, and practicing the professional skills you need to succeed in your career. While accelerating your career experience is a simple idea, it is not easy to apply.

Adopt the habit early in your career to make your own professional development a top priority by dedicating at least one hour per week. Over the course of one year, that weekly commitment will equal more than fifty hours. Very few professionals will develop that habit. Will you?

Practice the skills that you need for success with the dedication of a professional athlete, Hollywood actor, or a rock star. Most professional don't think about their jobs in this way, but practicing the skills that underlie your day-to-day work will pay off.

The most challenging part of implementing an approach as I am suggesting is the discipline to do so in the face of many other demands for your time. For me, the key to maintaining the discipline of a daily or weekly routine is to schedule it. Carve out a space in your calendar that you do not sacrifice. Another technique that may work for you is to commit to work on these skills with a friend or colleague.

The skills and concepts in *Career-ology* will be part of the foundation of your career. While you will use these skills more and less at different times in your career, they are all important. It is also very important to keep in mind that this book is only the beginning of a career-long journey of professional development. The truly successful professionals know that this journey is mostly self-guided and it is directed by a personal definition of success.

Early in the book, I emphasized that the people in your career matter and that they are the common thread for all of the skills and concepts presented in this book. It is worth repeating because the idea is so important. The people with whom you work—your colleagues, customers, clients, constituents, shareholders, patients, teammates, and partners—are the single most important element of your career. The quality of your relationships with people is directly related to your long-term career success.

Career-ology focuses on the skills related to communicating with people in written and spoken form. It teaches you how to persuade and influence people to adopt your viewpoint. The book also explains how to continuously develop and cultivate relationships with the people in your company and in your professional networks. *Career-ology* demonstrates the importance of understanding people and their roles in relation to your own. It teaches you how to begin to manage your personal brand. Finally, the book explains the concept of executive presence and introduces the idea of EI as it relates to work and career.

This is the start of your own professional development process. Good luck.

NEXT STEPS

1. Create your own career development plan that includes the skills in this book or another set of skills you identify. For it to be a plan, you must include specific outcomes or goals, a deadline, and first steps in order to get started.

2. Your career is yours. Do something—anything that moves your own professional development forward.

3. Connect with Career-ology. Tell us your story, share your experience, ask questions.

CONNECT WITH CAREER-OLOGY

There are many ways to connect. Explore www.career-ology.com, which includes the Link Library, a blog, new resources, book reviews, and exclusive online content.

Here are some other ways to connect with Career-ology:

Twitter—@jeffchapski keeps the conversation flowing on Twitter and features newly published articles, up-to-the minute news, and other cool stuff in 140 charters or less.

Facebook Page—convenes fellow Career-ologists who want to share their advice and experience, collaborate on ideas, and network with each other. https://www.facebook.com/careerologybook.

LinkedIn Group—hosts an exclusive (invitation only) group for Career-ologists who have successfully completed the Career-ology Workshop.

Email—jeff@career-olgy.com for your questions and feedback.

ACKNOWLEDGMENTS

Most grand endeavors in life require a team of people to succeeed. For me, writing this book has been a grand endeavor and I could not have done it without an outstanding team.

I would like to thank Sallie Randolph, John Randolph, and Catherine Carey at Librastream for their guidance, support, and expertise. They served as editors, proofreaders, production consultants, and idea collaborators. They are a pleasure to work with and I am deeply grateful for their dedication to this project. Thank you, Sallie, John, and Cathy.

It is ironic to say, "you can't judge a book by its cover" when referring to a book because cover design is a critical component of the finished product. Cindy Kiple did tremendous work in designing the cover and the interior layout. During the layout and production process, she was patient and accommodating in fine-tuning the design into the finished product you are holding in your hands. Thank you, Cindy.

In the digital age, a book has both a physical form and a digital one. The physical form is the one-hundred and fifty pages of paper between two glossy covers that rests on a bookshelf. The digital form of the book exists in many spheres including a WordPress blog, a Facebook page, a LinkedIn profile, and a Twitter account. I would like to thank Kate McMillan at Outbox Online Design Studio for her creative design talent and business acumen. It is rare to find both qualities in a single person. Thank you, Kate.

I would like to thank Phil Loeffler who provided feedback on the content and exceptional proof reading work. Your insight and careful attention to details helped make this a better book. Thank you, Phil.

This book would not have been possible without the writing contribution and expertise of Sherry Beck Paprocki. Thank, you Sherry.

Finally, I would like to thank Jennifer and Reid for all of their support and understanding during this project and for being a part of my most important team—my family.

ABOUT THE AUTHOR

Jeff Chapski has coached and mentored hundreds of college students and recent graduates as they started their first jobs and launched their careers. Recalling the important skills and lessons he learned early in his own career, Jeff started writing a blog at Career-ology.com to help new professionals succeed at work.

Jeff's first book, *Career-ology: The Art and Science of a Successful Career*, is based on twenty years of working with Fortune 100 companies and entrepreneurial start-ups in the financial services, consulting, and software sectors including: J.P. Morgan, Arthur Andersen, Bank of Tokyo, Chase Bank, Oracle Corporation, Hewlett-Packard, Microsoft, GE Capital, and TradeOut.com.

Jeff earned a degree in Finance from Georgetown University and currently serves on the Board of Directors of the Alumni Association. He is the founder of the Hoya Gateway program, co-founder of the Georgetown Entrepreneurship Alliance, and a member of the Board of Advisors for the Georgetown University Wall Street Alliance.

Jeff has lived and worked in the New York City metropolitan area for most of his career. He currently resides in Mamaroneck, New York with his wife and son. You can read Jeff's full bio at www.linkedin.com\jeffchapski or contact him via email at jeff@career-ology.com.